D1927854

Eysenck on Extraversion

H. J. EYSENCK

Eysenck on Extraversion

Crosby Lockwood Staples London

Granada Publishing Limited
First published in Great Britain 1973 by
Crosby Lockwood Staples, Frogmore, St Albans and
3 Upper James Street, London W1R 4BP

Printed in Great Britain by
Fletcher & Son Ltd, Norwich

ISBN 0 258 96910 5

ACKNOWLEDGEMENTS

Grateful acknowledgement for permission to reprint the articles in this volume is made to the following:

The editors of: *Acta Psychologica*, the *British Journal of Criminology*, the *British Journal of Psychiatry*, the *British Journal of Psychology*, the *Journal of Abnormal and Social Psychology*, the *Journal of Applied Psychology*, the *Journal of Experimental Research in Personality*, the *Journal of Social Psychology*, *Life Sciences*, *Occupational Psychology*, *Perceptual and Motor Skills*, the *Proceedings of the 18th International Congress of Psychiatry*, and to S. B. G. Eysenck, E. Howarth and R. Lynn.

CONTENTS

Part One:
The Nature of Extraversion

1

HISTORICAL INTRODUCTION

In 1947 I published my first book, *Dimensions of Personality* (Ref. 1), and in doing so took under my wing a most unattractive old thing with a caricature of a face—to wit, the concept of extraversion-introversion. In the long story of the development of the notions which finally crystallized into this conception there had never been a time when it had reached a lower point; the war years constituted a nadir from which most psychologists felt it would never rise again. To many, if not most, psychologists interested in personality it seemed as if I had attempted to resurrect a corpse—equivalent, perhaps, to trying to reintroduce into physics the notions of phlogiston, or aether, or a geocentric planetary system. This had many disadvantages, which will be only too obvious; no one wanted to read about extraversion, no one wanted to support research into this field, no one wanted to reconsider problems which were thought to be closed once and for all. But there were also compensating advantages, which may not be so obvious. Research is a rat race in which it is easy to fall behind; when you are the only one in the race you are left in peace to fashion your own theories, carry out your own researches, and reach your own conclusions without having to look over your shoulder constantly to see if others are catching up with you and perhaps overtaking you. If progress was slow, at least it was not forced; other researchers rode off in many other directions, often at much greater speeds, but it seemed possible that perhaps the right direction was more important than the greater speed.

In 1957, with the publication of *The Dynamics of Anxiety and Hysteria* (Ref. 2) the pace began to quicken. In this book I tried to take one step further the purely descriptive, factor analytic work that had formed the basis of my studies until then, and to attempt a theoretical unification of the experimental field in terms of concepts like inhibition and excitation, borrowed from learning theory—in particular, from Pavlov and Hull. Now other workers began to come into the field, and many reports appeared which confirmed—or, more frequently, disconfirmed—the hypotheses which I had worked out. Clearly the theory, while it might be on the right lines, was still quite inadequate to do justice to the known facts, or to make possible unambiguous prediction of facts hitherto unknown. Consequently work was begun on a third model, which saw the light in 1967 under the title of *The Biological Basis of Personality*

(Ref. 4); it is believed that this model is more satisfactory than either of the earlier ones, although of course still much in need of improvement, and in due course destined for the scrap-heap when it has served its purpose of stimulating sufficient research to make clearer its imperfections. This third model takes the notions of excitation and inhibition, which were previously used in a purely psychological sense, and attempts to translate them into physiological terms; this effort to link up with recent work on arousal and the reticular formation has made it possible to explain many previously inexplicable findings.

Altogether, I believe that an adequate understanding of the problems in this field, and the attempted solutions as well, is impossible without some knowledge of the history and the development of the psychological theories of personality. There are roughly speaking twelve periods of development, each associated with an outstanding personality whose work marked a definite advance; it may be useful if these twelve advances are defined in some detail. It is often said that psychology has a long past, but a short history; this is equally true of the study of personality. The moment when intuitive understanding, philosophical speculation and clinical intuition, which constituted the past, gave way to experimental study, psychological theory, and psychometric analysis can be defined more easily here than in most other areas of psychology; the turning point is associated with the extremely original and fundamental work of a man whose very name is probably unknown to most psychologists, even those who are actively working in the field of personality study. This man was the Dutch philosopher and psychologist G. Heymans (1857–1930) who published his views and results in book form in 1929 (Ref. 8) but who had written his fundamental papers (with E. Wiersma and H. Brugmans) some 20 years earlier. To him, appropriately, this book is dedicated; we shall see in a minute just why it is he, rather than others who are more often named and who are better known to psychologists, who may be said to mark the transition point from unscientific past to scientific history.

The story begins—if the human search for an understanding of personality, individual differences, temperamental peculiarities and other deviations from the strictly average sort of behaviour can in any real sense be said to have a 'beginning'—with Galen, a Greek physician who lived in the second century A.D. and who is widely credited with the enunciation of the doctrine of the four temperaments. The melancholic, the choleric, the sanguine and the phlegmatic, shorn of the associated theory of the 'humours' which were believed to cause their striking differences, have passed into every-day language, and the man in the street still uses these phrases in characterizing certain 'types' of behaviour. As we shall see, the theory of extraversion-introversion is intimately connected with this ancient theory, laughable only to those who do not realize that it embodies a large slice of excellent clinical observation, without which it would never have been accepted, or have lasted longer than any other psychological theory. This is not the place to go into the vexed question of Galen's originality in this respect, or to discuss possible prior claims of Hippocrates and others; I am not sufficiently expert to discuss these questions, and for the purposes of this book they are not of too great importance. The reader interested in the early development of these theories may with confidence turn to A. A. Roback's *Psychology of Character* (Ref. 10).

The second chapter of our story opens with the contribution made by the great German philosopher and scientist Immanuel Kant in his book on *Anthropologie* (Ref. 9), which was a kind of text-book of psychology and in which he brought up-to-date the doctrine of the four temperaments and popularized it and made it acceptable to philosophers, physicians, theologists and other learned men concerned with human personality. Eysenck & Eysenck (Ref. 5) have translated his descriptions of the traits characterizing the four temperaments, and have drawn attention to the close relationship between these descriptions and the results of modern factor-analytic work in this field; they also point out that the main difference between his views and more modern ones lies in his categorical conception of 'types' as being unchangeable and pure. A person belongs to one of these four groups; he cannot change his position, and there are no intermediate degrees. This notion of 'types' has been rightly criticized by modern American writers, but unfortunately they ascribe such views to more recent writers than Kant—writers who in fact do not hold them, like Jung and Kretschmer.

Modern typology parts company with Kant in this respect, and the person who took this important step of translating categorical types into continuous dimensions, and who thus marks our third epoch, was none other than W. Wundt. His contribution is discussed in some detail in one of the papers reprinted in section one of this book, and little need therefore be said here other than that he pointed out that cholerics and sanguinics both shared the characteristic of being *changeable*, while phlegmatics and melancholics were *unchangeable*; substitute 'extravert' and 'introvert' for changeable and unchangeable, and our modern theory (in its descriptive aspects) is born. Add that he considered a second dimension (emotionality—nowadays often labelled neuroticism, or instability) to be formed by the two emotional temperaments, i.e. the choleric and the melancholic, as opposed to the other two, who were considered by him unemotional, and you have a two-dimensional description, continuously variable, of personality, very much as it is given by recent writings of Cattell, Guilford, or the present writer. Wundt, like Heymans, is seldom if ever mentioned by English-speaking writers on personality, in spite of his very important contribution. (Ebbinghaus, too, wrote along rather similar lines.)

The fourth great contribution comes from O. Gross, a Viennese physician who attempted to give a physiological basis to the personality dimension of extraversion-introversion (not then so called, of course; Gross wrote at the beginning of the present century). He conceptualized mental and emotional processes in terms of a primary function, subserving sensation and perception, and a secondary function, which subserved the perseveration of primary processes; individuals differed according to the length of the secondary process—introverts had a long, extraverts a short secondary process. He showed in fascinating detail how this conception (which tied up with the newly proclaimed theories of perseveration of the memory trace, by Müller and Pilzecker) could be used to account for the personality traits of the two types posited. His physiology is of course entirely speculative, as he himself recognized; it is fascinating to see how he (and later on McDougall in a paper reprinted in section one) tried to invent something akin to the Ascending Reticular Activating System, and how both succeeded in describing (by deduction from behaviour) something which at that time was far beyond the ken of physiologists and neurologists. Truly, if the reticular formation had not been discovered, it had certainly been invented by psychologists anticipating later developments!

We come now to the fifth epoch, and to G. Heymans and his colleagues. His contribution is threefold, and in each of his innovations he anticipated a large and important area of research.

(1) *Psychometric.* Heymans was the first to realize the importance of quantifying the implicit relationships between traits which had served earlier writers; where they simply observed and noted subjectively 'what goes with what' (in Spearman's phrase), he suggested the use of correlational methods, and worked out a very crude and elementary, but nevertheless useful, coefficient of association. He also worked out methods of grouping such correlations, thus in essence anticipating factor analysis. He was not a gifted mathematician, and curiously enough

rejected product-moment correlation coefficients for quite the wrong reasons, but he did have an intuitive understanding of the logical requirements of mathematical analysis, and pioneered what are now widely used methods.

(2) *Experimental.* He was perhaps the first to realize that observation of every-day behaviour is not sufficient to build a science of personality on, and he carried out experimental studies to measure individual differences in behaviour; these are perhaps the first properly to deserve the name of 'experiments in personality'—Galton's studies, to take but one example that seems to disprove this generalization, were not experimental in the laboratory sense.

(3) *Hypothetico-deductive method.* He realized that science is intimately tied to the use of the hypothetico-deductive method, except perhaps in its first, tentative steps, and he linked the theories of Gross with his psychometric work and his experiments into a nomological network, to use a term which would have been new to him, but the implications of which were apparent in his work. These three major contributions entitle him to be called the father of experimental personality research; unfortunately his writings are widely dispersed and do not lend themselves to reproduction in this volume, but a description, with quotations, of his work has been given in *The Structure of Human Personality* (Ref. 3).

The next claimant for a place in our company of immortals is C. G. Jung, whose contribution to personality study is often misinterpreted. C. Spearman, in his classic *Abilities of Man* (Ref. 11), sums up the work of Heymans, Wiersma and Brugmans by saying:

> So far as scientific status is concerned, this Dutch work stands upon a very high plane. In it mere casual observations—shown over and over again to be grossly misleading—are replaced by most careful and systematic investigations.

He goes on to characterize Jung with equal insight:

> Ideas substantially the same as those mentioned above re-appeared not long afterwards in the work of Jung. But the arduous scientific research of his predecessors . . . now gives way to attractive literary embellishment.

Jung is often credited with giving a long list of other writers who preceded him in delineating his types of extraversion and introversion; it is interesting that although these types are so very similar to Heymans' carefully researched strong and weak secondary function types, yet Heymans is never mentioned—in spite of the fact that much of his work was published in German, and must have been familiar to Jung. If Jung's descriptions are not original, neither is his use of the terms extraversion and introversion; these had been used in European writings for several hundred years before him. His main claim to originality must be his suggestion that extraversion was linked with the hysterical group of neurotic disorders, introversion with the psychasthenic group (dysthymia—anxiety, reactive depression, phobias, obsessive-compulsive disorders). There appears to be some truth in this observation, and while the neurotic typology must be credited to Janet rather than to Jung, nevertheless the identification with normal personality types is important in the historical development of the concept.

Related to Jung in that his main concern was with the abnormal counterparts of normal personality types was E. Kretschmer, but his main contribution did not lie in his identification of extraversion ('cyclothymia') with manic-depressive insanity and introversion ('schizothymia') with schizophrenia (Jung too had thought of schizophrenia as being linked with introversion). The evidence does not suggest that schizophrenia does in fact have such a link; several papers are included in this volume demonstrating that such a generalization would not now be acceptable—although it must of course be realized that the term 'schizophrenia' means many things to many people, and that its use in modern Anglo-American psychiatry may not be identical with its use in German-speaking circles fifty years ago. However that may be, Kretschmer's continuing fame rests on his insistence on the importance of constitutional factors, and on his insight into the relationship between leptomorphic bodybuild and introversion. While again the evidence regarding bodybuild and insanity, on which he insisted so strongly, is at best inconclusive, there seems to be no doubt that in the normal field at least a relationship of the kind postulated by him exists—although much weaker than he (and Sheldon, who took up his system with minor modifications) believed. Correlations of 0·4 or thereabouts are the most that can be expected when the elementary errors in conducting such experiments which disfigure his and even more Sheldon's work are rectified. (Both Kretschmer and Sheldon contaminated their judgement of temperament and of diagnosis by knowledge of bodybuild of the subjects of their studies; this contamination produced unacceptably high correlations often exceeding the reliabilities of the ratings involved! Furthermore, Kretschmer took little trouble to partial out the effects of age; later work has shown this to be essential.) But constitutional factors are important, as we shall see, and Kretschmer was the first to insist on their importance.

The pace now quickens, and our epochs begin to overlap. After Jung, the next great writer to be noted is perhaps C. Spearman, the founder of the London School—a 'school to end schools', as he once put it, in an attempt to crystallize his belief that the method of factor analysis, which he introduced into psychology, was capable of substituting objective, quantitative fact for subjective, intuitive belief. Through his students (Webb, Garnett, Oates) and his collaborators and successors (notably Burt, Stephenson and Cattell) he exerted a profound influence, and while history remembers him more for his work in intelligence measurement, we must note here that he was the first to demonstrate the existence of the two factors, strictly defined and measured, of emotionality-neuroticism ('w' in his terminology) and of extraversion-introversion ('c' in his terminology). He also tried to elaborate experimental tests of perseveration, with which to measure these personality traits; these were unsuccessful, possibly because he and his students were thinking in terms of psychometric group tests, not in terms of experimental laboratory examinations, given to one person at a time. Whatever the defects of his work, viewed from the vantage point of hindsight, his contribution, substantive and methodological, was crucial in transplanting the Dutch work to English soil.

The contribution of our ninth great figure, J. P. Guilford, can best be understood in terms of the problem which he set out to solve. Briefly, the situation may be summarized by saying that the success of the Woodworth Neuroticism questionnaire, and the appearance of the English translation of Jung's book, inspired many psychologists in the U.S.A. to produce questionnaires of neuroticism and introversion respectively. The essentially subjective method used of picking out items and combining them in an essentially arbitrary fashion guaranteed that these 'measuring instruments' measured nothing in particular, and when it was found that neuroticism inventories intercorrelated only about 0·3, while neuroticism and introversion inventories showed correlations of equal size, it was concluded that this whole approach had been a failure. The bitter taste of this failure survived for a long time, without realization that it was not due to any faults in theoretical conceptualization or in the principle of questionnaire construction but rather to inadequacies in the make-up of these particular questionnaires. It is easy to see this now but at the time many psychologists vowed never again to use personality inventories and never again to think in terms of introversion-extraversion; in many cases this vow survived the Second World War and is only slowly losing its compulsive force. Guilford's great contribution was the realization that the intercorrelations between inventory items, and the factor analysis of these intercorrelations, constitute indispensable steps in the isolation of stable personality factors and the construction of suitable questionnaires; his pioneering work is suitably recognized by the inclusion in this book of one of his early papers. Guilford also contributed experimental studies which at the time were outstanding examples of the laboratory approach to personality study. If the findings were largely negative this was perhaps inevitable at the particular stage of development reached at that time by both personality theory and experimental psychology.

Our tenth author is the Russian writer B. M. Teplov, who has taken up the Pavlovian teaching with respect to the 'strong' and 'weak' nervous system, and has built upon this an impressive series of experimental studies of individual differences, ably recounted in English by J. Gray (Ref. 7). It has always seemed to me that Teplov's 'weak nervous system' is analogous to the introverted type, his ' strong nervous system' to the extraverted type; hence his inclusion in this list. A lengthy discussion of the points of similarity and difference between the two typologies by J. Gray is included in volume one of this book, so no more needs to be said on this point. It may be worth while, however, to point out the novelty and interest of many of the techniques pioneered by the Russian workers. The stereotyped choice by Western psychologists of such obviously poor measuring instruments as the Rorschach or the M.M.P.I. when called upon to investigate personality traits is put to shame by the inventive genius of the Moscow group. Perhaps only Cattell escapes this censure on our side of the fence, because he, too, has attempted (with considerable success) to break out of the bear-hug of tradition. The Russian work, too, has its weaknesses, of course, and these may loom larger to psychometric readers than its strengths but Teplov's successors are taking great strides to eliminate these weaknesses and the immediate future may benefit greatly from cross-fertilization.

We are now nearing the present day, and the work of our next exponent is still very much in progress. (Guilford, too, is of course still active at this writing, but his interest has shifted to the study of cognitive dimensions and originality.) R. B. Cattell has transferred the traditions of the London School to American soil, and has combined exceptional mastery of statistical techniques of multiple factor analysis with large-scale empirical studies employing ratings and self-ratings, and objective, experimental and physiological measurements of the most varied groups. This work goes well beyond the confines of our interests here but it should be noted that in all his groups the two factors (usually extracted as higher-order factors derived from the intercorrelations between oblique primary factors) of extraversion-introversion and neuroticism (called 'anxiety' by him) emerge more clearly and strongly than any others. As undoubtedly the foremost living exponent of the factor-analytic approach, this constant verification of the fundamental descriptive hypothesis on which much of the material in this book is based is most valuable and welcome, and the large area of factual agreement between him, Guilford, and the present writer on this point has been factually documented in great detail (Ref. 6).

Last, least, and only after much hesitation the writer would place his own contribution. In essence, what he has tried to do has been a continuation of the three-fold approach of the Dutch school, as adapted by Spearman and made by him a characteristic of the London school. Our psychometric work has been summarized extensively, with much new material, in *The Description and Measurement of Personality* (Ref. 5). Our experimental work has been similarly summarized in *The Dynamics of Anxiety and Hysteria* (Ref. 2) and later papers and writings. Our hypothetico-deductive approach can best be studied in *The Biological Basis of Personality* (Ref. 4), in which an attempt is made to deduce extravert-introvert differences in behaviour, both social and in the laboratory, in terms of differences in cortical arousal, mediated by the reticular formation. The success of these efforts is still too doubtful, and the work itself too recent, to comment on it in any detail; the reader will be able to judge for himself after perusal of the relevant articles reprinted in this volume.

Thirty years of work in this neck of the woods, and careful reading of documents straddling 2,000 years of historical development, have given rise to some general impressions which may be useful to newcomers to this field. In the first place, there is a strong feeling of historical continuity. Galen's and Kant's observations do not strike the modern observer as ridiculous and outmoded; our own work may be more extensive, better controlled and statistically more defensible, but it is recognizably a development of ideas mooted all these centuries ago. Gross's and Heymans' speculations about physiological mechanism have little factual substratum, but they are not out of line with what we now know about the structure of the cortico-reticular arousal loop, and its functioning. Spearman's and Guilford's early factorial studies are now very out-dated, but modern methods, aided by computers, do not give results essentially different from theirs. In fact, what we recognize throughout this historical development is the usual scientific progress, slow, step by step, brick by brick, until finally we arrive, almost by stealth, at a splendid, well-built usable structure. So many hands have made their contribution that it becomes difficult to say: *he* built it. All those who contributed have built it, although some have made a bigger contribution than others.

In the second place, there is a feeling that for a long time contributions were made by single people, or at best small groups; others were slow to take up the contributions made. Heymans' work has been followed up in Holland, and later in South Africa, but is hardly known elsewhere; even the recent work of Cattell is carried out mostly by his students and fellow-workers, not by the general body of research students. This position is slowly changing; gradually a more general approach is being elaborated in which theories are being tested in different laboratories all over the world.

A third point which may be important is that personality study is beginning to cease to be the prerogative of a small set of psychologists who happen to be interested in individual differences, while the great body of experimental and theoretical psychologists goes its own way, profoundly unmoved by whatever may be going on in this small corner. If extraverts and introverts differ in their habitual arousal level, as well as in their sensory thresholds, orienting reactions, adaptation rates, E.E.G., E.M.G. and G.S.R. response patterns, rates of conditioning, perceptual after-effects, and a thousand and one psychological and physiological measures, then it ceases to be practical for the experimentalist to proclaim his disinterest in 'personality' and relegate individual differences to the error term in his analysis of variance; interaction terms, embodying personality in the form of extravert-introvert differences, become extremely important and should be extracted from any well-planned study, even when personality differences are not the main point of interest. I have discussed this point at some length elsewhere (Ref. 4) and will not insist on it here to any greater length. It is my impression that the lesson is gradually being learned, and that more and more hard-bitten experimentalists are taking individual differences into account.

It is unfortunate in this connection that the terms extraversion and introversion are in many people's minds linked so closely with the putative father of this personality typology, C. G. Jung. From the point of view of scientific study, his contribution has been largely a negative one; by allowing his mystical notions to overshadow the empirical, observational data he has done his best to remove the concept of personality type from the realm of scientific discourse. His extremely complex system, involving four 'functions' arranged in contrasting pairs, all of which can be extraverted or introverted, and which compensate each other in a complex manner in which conscious extraversion may be linked with unconscious introversion, has not found much favour with even his more devoted followers; as he once pointed out when questioned on whether a given person was extraverted or introverted: 'In the last analysis I decide who is an extravert and who is an introvert!' This splendid assertion of faith mirrors Goering's famous statement when someone pointed that his personal favourite, *Luftwaffe* General Milch, was in fact Jewish: 'I decide who is a Jew!', but it will prove somewhat less attractive to scientists who attempt to construct a universal, objective science of personality structure and measurement. Psychologists will have to learn the plain historical fact that the personality types of extraversion and introversion owe very little to Jung, and the sooner this message reaches psychological textbooks, the better.

It is interesting that the first appearance of the term 'extraversion' in an English dictionary, appropriately enough, is in Dr Johnson's *Dictionary of the English Language*, which appeared in 1755; it does not tell us very much, however, as he defines it as 'the act of throwing out: the state of being thrown out'. J. A. H. Murray, in the *Oxford Dictionary* of 1897, quotes G. Coles (1692–1732) as having used the term in a rather more modern sense—'a turning of one's thoughts upon outward objects'. M. E. Lazarus, in his book *Love versus Marriage*, which was published in 1852 in New York, speaks of 'introversion, the turning inward of the being to act against himself. . . . The habit of introverted thoughts has very morbid tendencies and incapacitates us from appreciating the real values and beauties that surround us.' And in 1899, W. D. Whitney in his *Century Dictionary* defined introversion as 'the act of introverting, or the state, of being introverted; turning or directing inward, physical or mental'. Thus the terms themselves were current long before Jung's book appeared, and they were used with a meaning not too dissimilar to that which they have now assumed.

The model of personality which is implicit in the papers here reprinted is one which has often been criticized; it may be useful to point out that not all the criticisms are justified. It is suggested, for instance, that no model with two or three factors or dimensions only can possibly do justice to the complexity of human nature. True but irrelevant. It has never been asserted that extraversion and neuroticism are the *only* variables which affect human conduct, and produce individual differences in personality; it is merely asserted that they are *important* variables, and worthy of further study. We do not criticize the student of the physical properties of oxygen, say, or bismuth, for asserting that there was nothing in nature but oxygen, or bismuth. Nor is it the intention of the scientific investigator to follow the poet or dramatist in depicting human behaviour in all its aspects; being a scientist he sets himself limited goals, and asks to be judged in terms of his success in reaching these. We know very little, and hence our goals must necessarily be very limited indeed. To fail to recognize this is to fail to recognize the essential nature of scientific endeavour.

Another criticism asserts that there are many anomalies in the model, and that experiment has often failed to verify prediction. Again, the criticism is true but irrelevant. No scientific theory has ever been free of anomalies, and some of these have been quite obtrusive. Thus Newton had the greatest difficulties in fitting the moon into his planetary system, and failed completely to account for the aberrant motions of Mercury; even today we cannot account for these either in terms of his system, or in terms of Einstein's theory. Where even the best established theories show anomalies, it is not unexpected that a rather novel theory, dealing with some of the most complex sets of facts and concepts we know, should also do so. Specific criticisms of such anomalies, leading to improvements in the theory, are of course always welcome; general criticisms of the theory as a whole, because of specific anomalies, are rather beside the point.

A third type of criticism is often put in the form of raising doubts as to whether we are really measuring extraversion at all; how do we know, it is said, that we are not in fact dealing with some other entity altogether? Such a criticism is clearly misconceived, in that it reifies extraversion; it assumes that somewhere *out there* is something called extraversion, and that we can match our measures against this something and find out whether we have got the right test or not. Unfortunately this is nonsense; there is nothing *out there* against which we could compare our measures. Extraversion is a concept, like gravitation, or intelligence; concepts are man-made, and cannot claim any *real* existence, whatever that may mean. Such criticisms are naïve philosophically and meaningless scientifically; the question is not whether what we are measuring and experimenting with is extraversion, but whether what we are measuring and experimenting with is useful in understanding known facts and in predicting unknown ones. Semantic riddles are not of much concern to scientists.

The same answer applies to criticisms such as that according to the theory E and N are orthogonal, but that in some early studies with the M.P.I. negative correlations of 0·2 or thereabouts have been reported. Here again, there is the vague notion that somewhere out there we have two dimensions, E and N, and that these either are or are not orthogonal. But that, of course, is not the position at all; we are free to define and choose our concepts within certain broad limits, and it seems preferable to have orthogonal concepts where that is possible. The observed correlations between personality inventory scales reflect the particular choice of questions in these inventories; it is easy, by suitable choice, to make the correlation zero, +ve or −ve. In the E.P.I., which was drawn up to succeed the M.P.I. and to have orthogonal scores, suitable choice of questions did in fact produce orthogonal scores. These are problems of test construction, not questions of fact; the real point at issue is whether the resulting scales will be useful in producing scientific advances.

It is important to be clear about which parts of the theory are empirically testable, and which are part of the set of hypotheses which define the theory. Much fruitless discussion has been indulged in regarding the former type of question; it is hoped that the appearance of this volume of reprinted articles will serve to some extent to direct attention rather to the latter type of question. These articles are part of a larger three-volume edition of *Readings in Extraversion-Introversion*, containing contributions by many different authors; the inevitably high price of such a large collection, amounting to 1,400 pages in all, suggested the desirability of making available a rather smaller set of reprints in paper-back form for students and others ill-equipped to buy the larger set. To make the collection more complete, a few articles not contained in the original set have been added, and this introduction has been rewritten. It is hoped that this small collection will be found useful, and that it will whet the reader's interest in the fascinating field of study to which it is intended to be an introduction.

REFERENCES

1. EYSENCK, H. J., *Dimensions of Personality*. London: Routledge & Kegan Paul, 1947.
2. ——, *The Dynamics of Anxiety and Hysteria*. London: Routledge & Kegan Paul, 1957.
3. ——, *The Structure of Human Personality*. London: Methuen, 1970 (3rd Edition).
4. ——, *The Biological Basis of Personality*. Springfield, Ill.: Charles C. Thomas, 1967.
5. ——, and EYSENCK, S. B. G., *The Description and Measurement of Personality*. London: Routledge & Kegan Paul, 1969.
6. ——, and EYSENCK, S. B. G., On the unitary nature of extraversion. *Acta Psychol.*, 26, 383–390, 1967.
7. GRAY, J. A., *Pavlov's Typology*. Oxford: Pergamon Press, 1964.
8. HEYMANS, G., *Inleiding Tot de Speciale Psychologie*. Harlem: Bohn, 1929.
9. KANT, I., Anthropologie in pragmatischer hinsicht, in *Werke*, Vol. IV. Berlin: Bruno Cassirer, 1912–1918.
10. ROBACK, A. A., *The Psychology of Character*. London: Kegan Paul, 1927.
11. SPEARMAN, C., *The Abilities of Man*. London: Macmillan, 1927.

2

Principles and Methods of Personality Description, Classification and Diagnosis

H. J. EYSENCK

First published in *British Journal of Psychology*, **55,** 284–294, 1964

CLASSIFICATION is an absolutely fundamental part of the scientific study of human personality; a satisfactory typology is as necessary in psychology as was Mendeleev's table of the elements in physics (Ref. 17). This has, of course, always been recognized, and almost everyone is acquainted with the famous typological classification into melancholics, cholerics, sanguines and phlegmatics dating back to Galen and even earlier. As this system still has much to teach us, I shall present it as Fig. 1; the outer ring in this figure shows the results of a large number of factor analytic studies of questionnaires and ratings (Ref. 23). As is customary in these diagrams, the correlation between any two traits is equal to their scalar product, that is to say, in this case, the cosine of their angle of separation.

Fig. 1 immediately confronts us with some of the main problems of classification. The first of these may be phrased in terms of the question: 'Categorical or dimensional?' Kant, to whom this system owes much of its popularity during the last two hundred years, was quite specific in maintaining the categorical point of view, i.e. the notion that every person could be assigned to a particular category; he was a melancholic, or a phlegmatic, or a sanguine or a choleric, but any mixtures or admixtures were inadmissible. This notion of categories is, of course, similar to the psychiatric notion of disease entities and their corresponding diagnoses; hysteria, anxiety state, paranoia, obsessional illness, and so on, are often treated as categorical entities in this sense.

Opposed to this notion we have the view that any particular position in this two-dimensional framework is due to a combination of quantitative variations along the two continua labelled 'introversion-extraversion' and 'stable-unstable'. Wundt (Ref. 51), who is the most notable proponent of Galen's system in modern times, favours the dimensional view; he labelled the one axis 'slow-quick' instead of

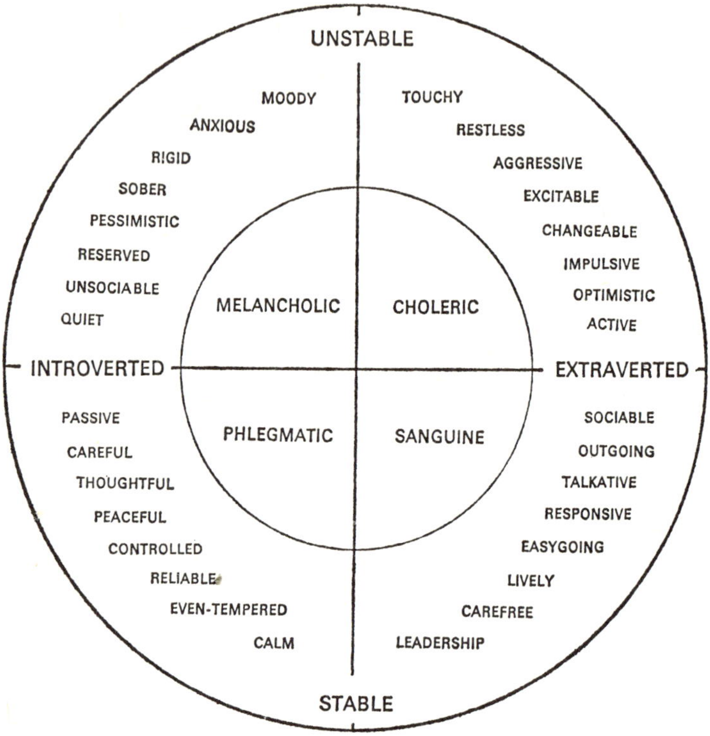

Figure 1. Diagram showing relation between the classical four temperaments and results of modern factor analytic methods of personality description.

'introversion-extraversion', and the other 'strong-weak' instead of unstable and stable.

It may be interesting to quote Wundt's very modern-sounding discussion:

> The ancient differentiation into four temperaments . . . arose from acute psychological observations of individual differences between people. . . . The fourfold division can be justified if we agree to postulate two principles in the individual reactivity of the affects: one of these refers to the strength, the other to the speed of change of a person's feelings. Cholerics and melancholics are inclined to strong affects, while sanguinics and phlegmatics are characterized by weak

ones. A high rate of change is found in sanguinics and cholerics, a slow rate in melancholics and phlegmatics.

It is well known that the strong temperaments . . . are predestined towards the *Unluststimmungen*, while the weak ones show a happier ability to enjoy life. . . . The two quickly changeable temperaments . . . are more susceptible to the impressions of the present; their mobility makes them respond to each new idea. The two slower temperaments, on the other hand, are more concerned with the future; failing to respond to each chance impression, they take time to pursue their own ideas (pp. 637, 638).

There is no reason to believe that the notion of a typology presupposes a categorical system; both Jung and Kretschmer, who were probably the best known typologists of the inter-war period, postulated a dimensional rather than the categorical system. The widespread notion that typologists imply discontinuities, bimodal distributions, and the like, does not accurately represent the writings and views of modern typologists.

Most writers on the subject of personality come down in favour of either the categorical or the dimensional point of view without basing themselves on any experimental demonstration. I have always felt that this is unwise and that it should not be impossible to devise experimental and statistical means for verifying the one and falsifying the other hypothesis. I have tried to do this in terms of the method of criterion analysis, which relies on separate factor analyses of intercorrelations between tests administered to two or more criterion groups (say normals and psychotics), and the comparison of the factors emerging with a criterion column derived by serial correlation between the tests and the criterion (Ref. 10). The results of this method have in every instance supported the doctrine of continuity, and failed to support the doctrine of categorization, even when the latter seemed most firmly entrenched, as in the case of psychosis (Ref. 12).

Assuming for the moment, therefore, the doctrine of dimensionality, we are required to build up on an experimental and statistical basis a quantitative system of personality description (Ref. 36). The most widely used tool for this purpose is, of course, factor analysis, and the main results of the application of this tool are shown in Fig. 1. It is notable that for many years factor analysis has been criticized because, so it was said, there was no agreement between factor analysts. Whatever may have been true twenty or thirty years ago, there can be no doubt that nowadays there is comparatively little disagreement between investigators in this field. Cattell's most recent book (Ref. 3) shows him in firm agreement with the system I first put forward in 1947 (Ref. 9), and Guilford, too, now appears to recognize the existence of these two main factors in personality description which I have used as the major axes in Fig. 1. Vernon (Ref. 49, p. 13) also puts forward a similar scheme. Equally we are all agreed that each of these factors is what Thurstone called a 'second-order factor', i.e. is extracted from the intercorrelations between 'first-order factors' or traits. It is with respect to these traits that much research is still needed before any final agreement is reached. Nevertheless, the major outlines of the picture are certainly beginning to appear, and it is notable that this agreement has been reached between workers using different premises, different factor analytic methods, different subjects, different tests and questionnaires, and different methods of rotation.

If we accept the principle of continuity, then we should be able to find a place for the major psychiatric classification of neurotic disorders within our Fig. 1. The theory has been put forward that neurotics suffering from anxiety, reactive depression, obsessions, phobias, and so on, would be found in the 'melancholic' quadrant, while hysterics and psychopaths would be found in the 'choleric' quadrant; psychotics would lie on an axis orthogonal to both E and N (Ref. 11). Descriptively there seems little doubt about the truth of this hypothesis at least as regards the neurotic groups; it is only necessary to look at the traits characterizing people in these two quadrants to realize that they might almost have been quoted from a psychiatric text-book, rather than being the result of factor analytic studies of normal people. Nevertheless, more experimental support would seem to be required. Such support, in so far as it is based purely on descriptive measures, does not remove us from some of the difficulties implied in the use of the factor analytic method. It has often been shown, as for instance in the literature deriving from the Maudsley Personality Inventory (Ref. 41), that hysterics, psychopaths and various dysthymic groups are in fact all high on neuroticism or emotionality, but are differentiated very significantly with respect to extraversion and introversion.

However, on a more fundamental level we may still be bothered by what is in fact the second major problem posed by our Fig. 1. This problem relates to the exact position of the axes. Mathematicians and statisticians would agree that it is perfectly legitimate to use scalar products to indicate the relative position of two traits in the dimensional space indicated in Fig. 1, and they would also agree that the position of the traits can be legitimately referred to any two arbitrary axes drawn at right-angles in the plane. They would not, however, agree with the claim sometimes made that the position of these axes can be determined in any but an arbitrary or trivial sense by statistical or mathematical considerations alone, as is suggested by many psychologists, particularly in the United States. I have always agreed with this criticism and have tried to argue that by retaining purely statistical criteria of axes psychologists have got themselves separated off from the main body of experimental psychology, and have remained cocooned within a small tail-chasing system incapable of generating hypotheses that could be falsified (Refs. 13, 14, 15 & 19). What then is the answer to this problem?

My suggestion would be that a purely descriptive system in science inevitably must carry the burden of subjectivity, and that it is because they have only been interested in description that factor analysts have failed to make a major impact on psychology. What is required, so I would maintain, is a set of theories linking the major aspects of the descriptive system to causal theories which would be capable of falsification (Ref. 21). As an example of what I have in mind I may perhaps mention the set of theories relating introversion to heightened cortical excitation and lowered cortical inhibition. This enables us to make large numbers of predictions of an experimental nature which are unlikely to be verified unless both the descriptive and the causal systems, and the relations specified to exist between them, are in fact in some degree related to reality. Many such predictions have in fact been made, and the great majority have been verified; I may refer in this connection to hypotheses such as that extraverts, as compared with introverts, would be more difficult to condition, have larger reminiscence scores, have greater pain tolerance but less tolerance for sensory deprivation, are more subject to satiation, have lower sedation thresholds, have greater alpha frequency and amplitude on the EEG, more involuntary rest pauses during massed practice, have poorer vigilance, have greater speed/accuracy ratios, shorter after-images, and so forth.

This differentiation between descriptive and causal is of course related to that between phenotypic and genotypic, first made in the personality field by Pavlov on the basis of some of his animal experiments. (For a discussion of Pavlov's views and their development, Teplov's very interesting account may be consulted with advantage; it is available in English together with a detailed evaluation of recent Russian work in the personality field (Ref. 39).) I have tried to indicate the difference, from the point of view of personality structure, in Fig. 2; a detailed discussion of this point is given elsewhere (Ref. 24). In this diagram, the subscripts 'C' and 'B' refer to constitution and behaviour respectively; 'E' refers to environmental influences. It will be seen that at the most fundamental

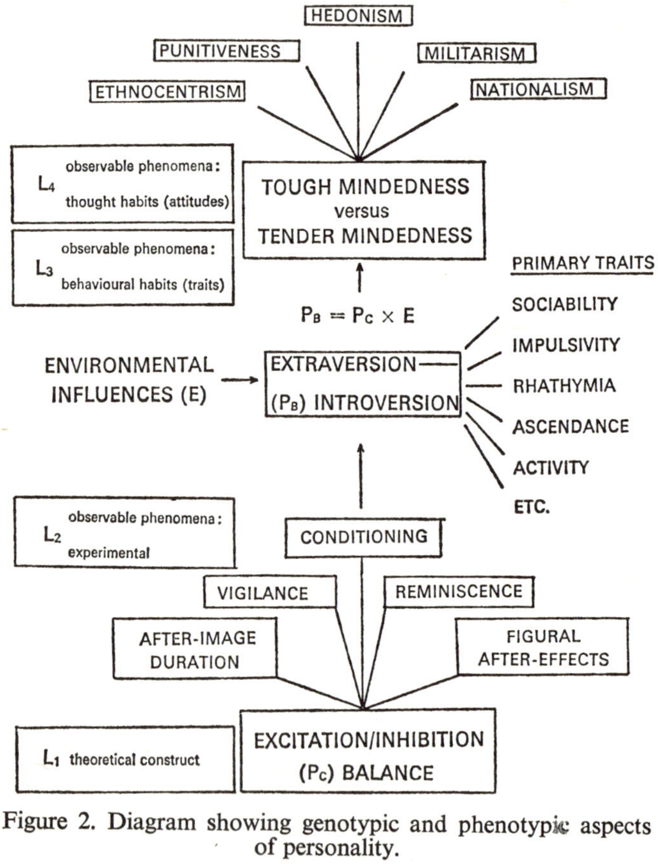

Figure 2. Diagram showing genotypic and phenotypic aspects of personality.

level we have the constitutional concept of the excitation/inhibition balance, which may be tilted in one direction or the other to give rise to constitutional, genotypic differences in extraversion-introversion; these may with some degree of accuracy be measured in terms of conditionability, vigilance, figural after-effects and other laboratory phenomena. Observable behaviour is a function of these constitutional differences in interaction with the environment; this interaction gives rise to descriptive, phenotypic differences in extraversion-introversion, which can best be measured in terms of questionnaires such as the M.P.I.[1]

We can now make deductions from these various postulates which enable us to perform critical experiments taking us out of the narrow circle of factor analysis altogether, and which make possible the use of the much more powerful techniques of multiple discriminant function analysis. Consider the following experiment in which sixteen normal subjects, sixteen dysthymics and sixteen hysterics were given a battery of six tests, selected on the basis of the causal theory outlined above (Ref. 33). We can predict, of course, how each group shall score as compared with the others, but we can go further than that. Our theory predicts that, if we carry out a discriminant function analysis, this should give us two significant latent roots; it can further be predicted that if we derive variate scores for the forty-eight subjects of our experiment, they should be situated in a prescribed manner in a two-dimensional plane generated by the two significant variates. To put this prediction in its simplest form we may say that the mean variate scores for the three groups should lie at the corners of an equilateral triangle.

Fig. 3 shows the outcome of the experiment. It will be seen that the prediction is verified, and that the first variate discriminates completely between the dysthymics and the hysterics. The second variate, with only slight overlap, discriminates between the normal group on the one hand and the two neurotic groups on the other.

Even where a causal hypothesis is not available it is often possible to use discriminant function analysis to decide between two hypotheses regarding the description of personality. Consider two hypotheses very frequently advanced regarding the neurotic and psychotic disorders (Ref. 18). Psychoanalysts often advocate the one-dimensional hypothesis; most psychiatrists, however, nowadays favour a two-dimensional hypothesis. A crucial test can, therefore, be devised involving the

[1] It seems reasonable to suppose that genotypic differences will ultimately be linked up with observable structural differences by physiologists and neurologists: an attempt to frame certain hypotheses of a testable character along these lines has been made by Eysenck (Ref. 30), who suggests that different parts of the ascending reticular formation may be implicated in the precise balance of the excitation/inhibition system. The effects of stimulant and depressant drugs on personality (Ref. 31) can also be brought into line by the assumption that the ascending reticular formation is concerned most intimately with the psychological constructs of excitation and inhibition.

dimensionality of the performance of the three groups on a battery of tests selected on the basis of some hypothesis regarding their relevance to neurotic and psychotic disorder (Ref. 18). In the actual experiment 20 normal controls, 20 neurotics and 20 psychotics were tested on four objective laboratory tests. Multiple discriminant function analysis disclosed two significant latent roots, thus rendering impossible the

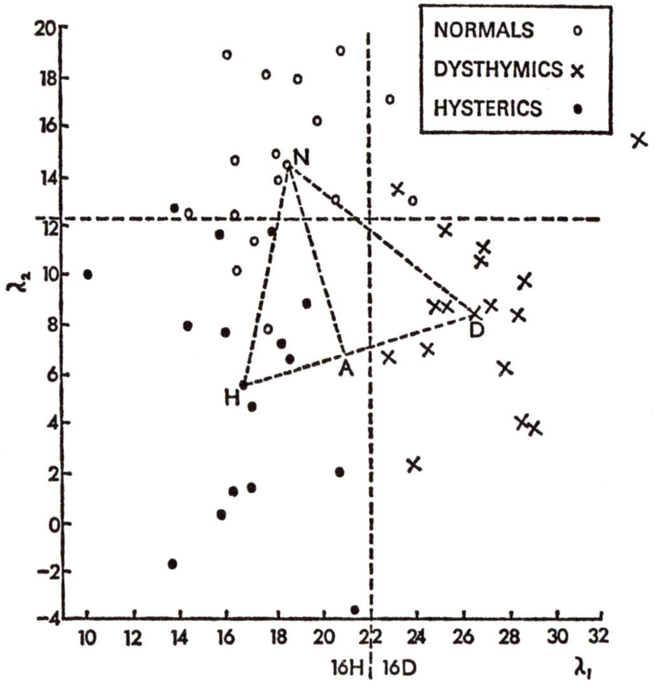

Figure 3, Position of 16 normal, 16 dysthymic and 16 hysteric subjects in two-dimensional space generated by multiple discriminant function analysis.

assumption that one dimension was sufficient to incorporate the results. Fig. 4 shows the actual positions of the members of the three groups; the correlation ratio between the three groups and the two variates was 0·84, which indicates a refreshingly high validity for the tests used in predicting these psychiatric criteria. That this figure is not higher is probably due to lack of reliability of the criteria; it will be seen in Fig. 4 that two of the neurotics, labelled A and B, were grouped with the psychotics by the tests. Both were readmitted later and diagnosed as psychotic.[1]

There are other ways in which theories of this type can be tested. One of these is the genetic method. If it is true that psychotic and neurotic disorders are orthogonal to each other, then we would expect that the children of psychotic parents should not show any greater degree of neuroticism than would the children of normal parents. This very

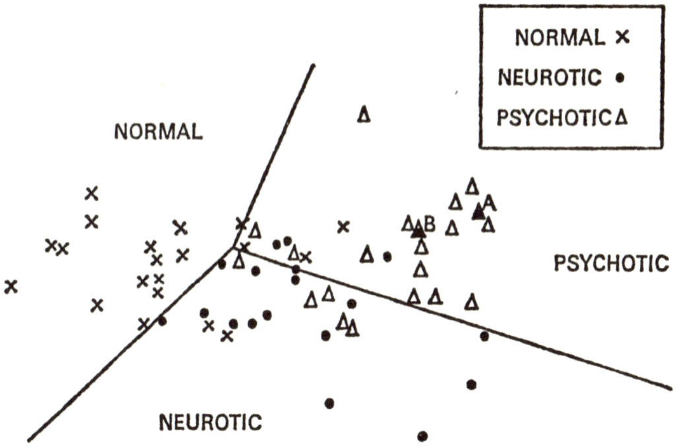

Figure 4. Diagram showing position of 20 normal, 20 neurotic and 20 psychotic subjects in two-dimensional space generated by multiple discriminant function analysis.

interesting hypothesis was tested by Cowie (Ref. 7) and her results leave no doubt that the genetic implication of neuroticism in the children of psychotic parents is non-existent; if anything they tended to be less neurotic! This finding may also serve as a warning to those who would overstress the importance of environment in giving rise to neurotic disorders; it is difficult to imagine a more severe stress to a child than having psychotic parents. In line with a generally hereditary view of the main dimensions of personality are also the results of a recent study of identical twins brought up in separation; in this work Shields (Ref. 46) found high correlations between the two twins for both extraversion and

[1] It is interesting that cultural differences do not seem to affect the applicability of method or conclusion to any considerable extent. Devadasan (Ref. 8) has duplicated many of the details of S. B. G. Eysenck's (Ref. 35) study in this field on an Indian population in Kerala (Trivandrum) with almost identical results.

neuroticism; he also found that these correlations were, if anything, higher than corresponding ones for identical twins brought up together! This type of proof which agrees well with previous studies by Eysenck & Prell (Ref. 34), Wilde (Ref. 50), Lienert & Reisse (Ref. 43) and many others, is relevant for the following reason. If we locate our axes in a random fashion, or according to some erroneous hypothesis, then we would not expect measures based on these placements to achieve any kind of biological reality. However, it has been amply demonstrated that extraversion, neuroticism and psychoticism show a powerful independent hereditary determination; it would seem to follow that the location of our axes cannot be random but must be at least to some degree in the right direction.

The last type of argument and proof, which I would suggest as appropriate, relates to the working out of aetiological models, and the design of methods of treatment related to these. It is a basic principle of behaviour therapy that neurotic disorders are simply maladaptive habits, acquired through a process of conditioning; or alternatively socially desirable habits which have failed to be acquired (Refs. 25 and 32). This hypothesis has led to much work relating dysthymic disorders to over-quick conditionability of patients, and hysteric and psychopathic disorders to chronic underconditionability of patients. (It will be remembered that overconditionability and underconditionability, respectively, are related to introversion and extraversion.) Support has already been brought forward to sustain these hypotheses, but I would be the last to claim that the case has, in any definitive sense, been proven; many points remain to be clarified and settled. The theory has, nevertheless, succeeded in giving rise to a method of treatment—behaviour therapy—which has been outstandingly successful as compared with previous methods. Again I will not claim too much for these new methods, and I will not go into the large and growing literature in any great detail, except to point out that success of treatment, if this is based on a definite theory, must to some degree strengthen the claim of that theory to be taken seriously. I would suggest, therefore, that aetiology and treatment must be taken into account in arriving at a final view of the adequacy of any principles of psychiatric classification claiming to be taken seriously.

The main points to emerge from this discussion are perhaps these. Factor analysis, principal component analysis, or some such technique, is necessary but not sufficient for the elaboration of a proper system of personality classification. The results achieved are inevitably subject to a large degree of subjectivity, and it is in principle impossible to avoid this subjectivity by statistical or mathematical manipulations. The descriptive results of factor analysis require to be integrated with causal theories relating to the factors tentatively established or indicated. It is only when these causal theories are tested and verified that the descriptive scheme can be accepted as forming part of the large body of data which make up experimental psychology.

There are, of course, many types of causal hypotheses which can be put forward in different situations, and there are many different types of deductions which can be made. It has been our task in this paper to touch in passing on several such causal hypotheses and deductions, and to show that the resulting picture is a reasonably congruent one which integrates observations, data, theories and experiments from a great variety of sources. There is, of course, no single proof of a theory such as the one here advocated, and no possibility of a crucial experiment; the burden of proof must lie in the general strength of the nomological network, linking together all these factors. It is believed that in this way psychiatric classification can be made much more reliable, valid and useful than it has been in the past when it relied exclusively on subjective observation, non-quantitative argument and non-experimental demonstration. Obviously the procedure of making our typologies more scientific has only just begun, and still has a long way to go before we can hope to achieve a satisfactory level of accuracy, reliability and validity; nevertheless, the success which has attended our first faltering steps does suggest that the method followed is the correct one and will in due course lead to a better understanding as well as to a better description of human behaviour and personality.

REFERENCES

1. BROWN, F. W., Heredity in the psychoneuroses. *Proc. R. Soc. Med.* **35,** 785–90, 1942.
2. CATTELL, R. B., *Factor Analysis.* New York: Harper, 1952.
3. —— & SCHEIER, I. H., *The Meaning and Measurement of Neuroticism and Anxiety.* New York: Ronald, 1961.
4. CLARIDGE, G. S., The excitation-inhibition balance in neurotics. In *Experiments in Personality*, vol. II, ed. H. J. Eysenck. London: Routledge & Kegan Paul, 1960.

5. ——, Arousal and inhibition as determinants of the performance of neurotics. *Brit. J. Psychol.*, **52,** 53–63, 1961.
6. —— & HERRINGTON, R. N., Sedation threshold, personality and the theory of neurosis. *J. ment. Sci.*, **106,** 1568–1583, 1960.
7. COWIE, V., The incidence of neurosis in the children of psychotics. *Acta Psychiat. Scand.*, **37,** 37–87, 1961.
8. DEVADASAN, K., Personality dimensions: a critical study. Ph.D. Thesis. University of Kerala, India, 1963.
9. EYSENCK, H. J., *Dimensions of Personality.* London: Routledge & Kegan Paul, 1947.
10. ——, Criterion analysis—an application of the hypothetico-deductive method to factor analysis. *Psychol. Rev.*, **57,** 38–53, 1950.
11. ——, *The Scientific Study of Personality.* London: Routledge & Kegan Paul, 1952.
12. ——, Schizothymia-cyclothymia as a dimension of personality. II: Experimental, *J. Pers.*, **20,** 345–384, 1952.
13. ——, Uses and abuses of factor analysis. *Appl. Statistics*, **1,** 45–49, 1952.
14. ——, The logical basis of factor analysis. *Amer. Psychologist*, **8,** 105–114, 1953.
15. ——, A psychological approach to the problem of non-uniqueness in multi-variate solutions. *Proc. Conference on Multi-Dimensional Analysis*, 24–27. Ann Arbor: Univ. of Michigan Press, 1954.
16. ——, Zur Theorie der Personlichkeitsmessung. *Z. diag. Psychol. Personlichkeitsf.*, **2,** 87–101, 171–187, 1954.
17. ——, Abord statistique et experimental du problème typologique dans la personalité neurotique, psychotique et normale. *L'Évolution psychiatrique*, **3,** 377–404, 1954.
18. ——, Psychiatric diagnosis as a psychological and statistical problem. *Psychol. Rep.*, **1,** 3–17, 1955.
19. ——, L'analyse factorielle et le problème de la validité. *Colloques int. Cent. nat. Rech. sci.*, Paris, **58,** 237–252, 1956.
20. ——, The questionnaire measurement of neuroticism and extraversion. *Riv. Psicol.*, **50,** 113–140, 1956.
21. ——, *The Dynamics of Anxiety and Hysteria.* London: Routledge & Kegan Paul, 1957.
22. ——, *Manual of the Maudsley Personality Inventory.* London: Univ. of London Press, 1959.
23. ——, *The Structure of Human Personality.* London: Methuen, 1960.

24. ——, Levels of personality, constitutional factors and social influences: an experimental approach. *Int. J. soc. Psychiat.*, **6,** 12–24, 1960.
25. ——, *Behaviour Therapy and the Neuroses.* Oxford: Pergamon Press, 1960.
26. ——, *Experiments in Personality*, ed. H. J. Eysenck. London: Routledge & Kegan Paul, 1960.
27. ——, Classification and the problem of diagnosis. In *Handbook of Abnormal Psychology*, ed. H. J. Eysenck. London: Pitman Medical, 1960.
28. ——, Personality and social attitudes. *J. Soc. Psychol.*, **53,** 243–248, 1961.
29. ——, Correspondence. *Brit. J. Psychol.*, **53,** 455–456, 1962.
30. ——, Biological basis of personality. *Nature*, **199,** 1031–1034, 1963.
31. ——, *Experiments with Drugs*, ed. H. J. Eysenck. Oxford: Pergamon Press, 1963.
32. ——, *Experiments in Behaviour Therapy*, ed. H. J. Eysenck. Oxford: Pergamon Press, 1963.
33. —— & Claridge, G., The position of hysterics and dysthymics in a two-dimensional framework of personality description. *J. abnorm. soc. Psychol.*, **69,** 46–55, 1962.
34. —— & Prell, P., The inheritance of neuroticism: an experimental study. *J. ment. Sci.*, **97,** 441–465, 1951.
35. Eysenck, S. B. G., Neurosis and psychosis: an experimental analysis. *J. ment. Sci.*, **102,** 517–529, 1956.
36. ——, Eysenck, H. J. & Claridge, G., Dimensional personality, psychiatric syndromes and mathematical models. *J. ment. Sci.*, **106,** 581–589, 1960.
37. Foulds, G. A., The logical impossibility of using hysterics and dysthymics as criterion groups in the study of introversion and extraversion. *Brit. J. Psychol.*, **52,** 385–387, 1961.
38. Franks, C. M., Souieff, M. I. & Maxwell, A. E., A factorial study of certain scales from the MMPI and the STDCR. *Acta Psychol.*, **17,** 407–416, 1960.
39. Gray, J. A., *Pavlov's Typology: Recent Theoretic and Experimental Works from the Laboratory of B. M. Teplov*, ed. J. A. Gray. Oxford: Pergamon Press, 1964.
40. Hildebrand, H. P., A factorial study of introversion-extraversion. *Brit. J. Psychol.*, **49,** 1–11, 1958.

41. KNAPP, R. R., *The Maudsley Personality Inventory Manual.* San Diego, California: Educational and Industrial Testing Service, 1962.

42. LAWLEY, D. N. & MAXWELL, A. E., Factor analysis as a statistical method. *The Statistician,* **12,** 209–229, 1962.

43. LIENERT, G. & REISSE, H., Ein korrelativer-analytischer Beitrag zur genetischen Determination des Neurotismus. *Psychol. Beiträge,* **7,** 121–130, 1961.

44. MCGUIRE, R. J., MOWBRAY, R. M. & VALLANCE, R. C., The Maudsley Personality Inventory used with psychiatric inpatients. *Brit. J. Psychol.,* **54,** 157–166, 1963.

45. SHAGASS, C. & NAIMAN, J., The sedation threshold as an objective index of manifest anxiety in psychoneurosis. *J. psychosom. Res.,* **1,** 49–57, 1956.

46. SHIELDS, J., Monozygotic twins brought up apart and brought up together. *An Investigation into the Genetic and Environmental Causes of Variation in Personality.* London: Oxford Univ. Press, 1962.

47. THOMSON, G. H., *The Factorial Analysis of Human Ability,* 5th ed. Univ. of London Press, 1951.

48. THURSTONE, L. L., *Multiple Factor Analysis.* Chicago: Univ. Press, 1947.

49. VERNON, P. E., *Personality Tests and Assessments.* London: Methuen, 1953.

50. WILDE, G. J. S., *Neurotische Labiliteit gemeten volgens de Vrangenlijstmethode.* Amsterdam: Uitg. F. van Rossen, 1962.

51. WUNDT, W., *Grundzüge der physiologischen Psychologie.* 5th ed., vol. 3. Leipzig: W. Engelmann, 1903.

3

A Short Questionnaire for the Measurement of Two Dimensions of Personality

H. J. EYSENCK

First published in *Journal of Applied Psychology*, **42,** 14–17, 1958

IN a previous paper, the writer has described the construction of two 24-item questionnaires for the measurement of neuroticism and extraversion (Ref. 2). The studies described in this paper were based on item analyses of some 250 questions appearing in well-known inventories, as well as a factor analysis of the finally chosen 48 questions, carried out separately for 200 men and 200 women. The reliabilities of the new questionnaires were reasonably high, in spite of their relative shortness, being 0·88 for neuroticism and 0·83 for extraversion. The independence of the two scales was demonstrated by the low correlation of −0·09 for the original sample of 400 men and women and the even lower correlation of −0·07 for a further male group of 200. Factorially, too, the items chosen for the two scales fell into two clearly separated groups making rotation to simple structure easy. A limited number of validation studies have been carried out and are quoted in *The Dynamics of Anxiety and Hysteria* (Ref. 3).

For many practical purposes, such as work in market research, for instance, even a relatively short questionnaire containing 48 questions may be too long, and the present study was designed to investigate the possibility of using an even shorter version containing only 6 questions for each of the two scales.

SUBJECTS AND METHOD

The subjects of the investigation were approached on a quota sample basis by the interviewers of one of the largest and most experienced British Market Research Organizations; these interviews are carried out all over England, correct proportions of urban and rural dwellers and of the different regions of the country being ensured. In addition to sex, the sample was divided according to age, 35 being the dividing line. Social class was assessed in the usual manner, the dividing line being taken between classes A, B and C on the one side and D and E on the other.

The total sample consisted of 1,600 subjects, divided into 8 groups of 200 each on the basis of the three selection criteria taken in all possible combinations. The reliability of sex and age classifications is known to be reasonably high; that for class is rather low (Ref. 1). We may expect these unreliabilities to lead to a varying degree of attenuation in our results.

In the interview, a number of questions were first asked relating to a variety of commercial products; these constituted the ostensible purpose of the interview. A few personal questions about age and occupation followed and finally the interview was terminated with the 12-item personality questionnaire given below. The questions were asked by the interviewer and the answers written down by him. The proportion of subjects approached who refused outright was 7 per cent; the proportion of subjects who consented to answer the questions in the first part of the interview and refused to answer the questions in the personality inventory was only 2 per cent.

The questions used in the study are given in Table 1. Each question answered 'Yes' was scored plus one point for neuroticism (marked 'N' in the key) or extraversion (marked 'E' in the key); each question answered 'No' was scored minus one point for neuroticism or extraversion, respectively, as shown in the key. No points were given for answers which could not be clearly classified as either 'Yes' or 'No' by the interviewer. The possible range of scores on either factor is therefore from plus six points to minus six points, a total of twelve points.

RESULTS

Tetrachoric correlations were run between the twelve questions and the resulting table of correlations factor analysed. Thurstone's procedure was followed and the two highly significant factors emerging were rotated in accordance with the principle of simple structure (Ref. 4). Table 2 gives the factor loadings of the rotated factors. Also given in Table 3 are the loadings of the 12 items which they had originally had in the analyses carried out on the whole population of 200 men and 200 women for all 48 items (Ref. 2). The comparison shows that the figures are remarkably similar from one occasion to the other, although methods of selection have changed considerably and although in the original analyses the 12 items were only a small part of the total number of items factor analysed. In some ways the new set of factor loadings is even more clear-cut than the original one. None of the E items has loadings on N as large as 0·10 and none of the N items has loadings on E as large as 0·10; in the original study several loadings exceeded this figure. We may conclude, then, that the factor structure has stood up well to repetition.

The correlation between extraversion and neuroticism is −0·05; this is very similar to the correlations reported previously for our samples of men and women. Again, therefore, the figures from the present study bear out in an important direction the conclusions from the original work. The split-half reliabilities (corrected) are 0·79 for N and 0·71 for E; these values are acceptable for group comparisons. (Test-retest reliabilities on small groups have been found to be slightly, but not significantly, in excess of these figures.)

Results of an analysis of variance for neuroticism and extraversion scores respectively are reported in Tables 3 and 4. Significant differences due to some of the main effects appear in the scores for both factors, but they are more conspicuous on the N scores, where they account for 7·41 per cent of the total variance, than on the E scores, where they only

TABLE 1

Questions	Key (+1 Yes, −1 No)
A. Do you sometimes feel happy, sometimes depressed, without any apparent reason?	N
B. Do you prefer action to planning for action?	E
C. Do you have frequent ups and downs in mood, either with or without apparent cause?	N
D. Are you happiest when you get involved in some project that calls for rapid action?	E
E. Are you inclined to be moody?	N
F. Does your mind often wander while you are trying to concentrate?	N
G. Do you usually take the initiative in making new friends?	E
H. Are you inclined to be quick and sure in your actions?	E
I. Are you frequently 'lost in thought' even when supposed to be taking part in a conversation?	N
J. Would you rate yourself as a lively individual?	E
K. Are you sometimes bubbling over with energy and sometimes very sluggish?	N
L. Would you be very unhappy if you were prevented from making numerous social contacts?	E

TABLE 2

Item	Present Sample		Original Sample			
	E	N	E_m	N_m	E_f	N_f
A	0·01	0·75	−0·10	0·79	−0·05	0·72
B	0·48	0·01	0·70	−0·09	0·73	0·03
C	−0·06	0·74	0·03	0·82	0·08	0·58
D	0·59	0·04	0·59	0·12	0·66	0·10
E	−0·09	0·71	−0·04	0·75	0·04	0·69
F	0·02	0·58	−0·13	0·57	0·00	0·50
G	0·59	−0·06	0·72	−0·15	0·66	0·14
H	0·49	−0·04	0·58	−0·09	0·51	−0·04
I	−0·06	0·58	−0·06	0·67	−0·03	0·59
J	0·68	−0·02	0·87	−0·05	0·65	−0·16
K	0·09	0·63	0·23	0·55	0·17	0·43
L	0·64	0·09	0·67	0·03	0·58	−0·08

TABLE 3

ANALYSIS OF VARIANCE OF THE NEUROTICISM SCORES

Source of Variance	Sum of Squares	df	m.s.v.
Total	20269·7775	1599	
Main effects			
Sex	995·4025	1	995·4025*
Class	311·5225	1	311·5225*
Age	142·8025	1	142·8028*
First order interactions			
Sex: Class	36·6025	1	
Sex: Age	0·0225	1	
Class: Age	1·3225	1	
Second order interactions	14·8225	1	
Totals			
All interactions	52·7700	4	13·1925
All differences between groups	1502·4975	7	214·6425
Residual variance within groups	18767·2800	1592	11·7885

* Signifies statistical significance at 5 per cent level.

TABLE 4

ANALYSIS OF VARIANCE OF THE EXTRAVERSION SCORES

Source of Variance	Sum of Squares	df	m.s.v.
Total	14263·8975	1599	
Main effects			
Sex	79·2100	1	79·2100*
Class	16·8100	1	16·8100
Age	28·6225	1	28·6225
First order interactions			
Sex: Class	3·4225	1	
Sex: Age	4·0000	1	
Class: Age	1·2100	1	
Second order interaction	0·9025	1	
Totals			
All interactions	9·5350	4	2·3838
All differences between groups	134·1775	7	19·1682
Residual variance within groups	14129·7200	1592	8·8755

* Signifies statistical significance at 5 per cent level.

account for 0·94 per cent. The sex difference is the greatest in relation to N and the only significant one in relation to E. On N, the women have a score roughly ½ SD higher than the men (i.e., women are less stable); on E, the men have a score roughly ⅙ SD higher than the women (i.e., men are more extraverted). Class and age differences are also significant for N, the lower class and younger age groups being slightly more unstable emotionally by ⅓ SD and ⅕ SD, respectively. None of the interactions give rise to mean square variances significantly greater than the residual error; on the whole they tend to be small. In fact, most of the observed differences are slight and only significant because of the large number of cases; little psychological importance would appear to attach to any of them except the sex difference on N, which is large and in line with previous work (Ref. 2).

The mean scores for N and E, respectively, are 0·15 and 1·96 for our sample; corrections for different proportions in the total populations would not give appreciably different estimates of population parameters and would appear to be a task of supererogation. Distributions of scores are sufficiently normal to permit the use of correlational statistics,[1] and the variances of the different groups are sufficiently

[1] The distribution of the E scores has a noticeable negative skew, but it is doubtful if this is sufficient to make desirable the use of logarithmic or other types of transformation.

homogeneous to permit analysis of variance to be carried out without transformation. The variances for N are slightly higher than those for E, being 11·73 as compared with 8·83.

A question regarding drinking habits was included in the questionnaire. A division was made between 'drinkers', i.e., those who drank frequently or sometimes and 'non-drinkers', i.e., those who drank very rarely or never. The N scores of these two groups were very similar, being −0·37 as compared with 0·04; if anything, it appears that 'non-drinkers' as here defined are very slightly more unstable than drinkers. The small size of the difference does not warrant our taking this conclusion too seriously. The E scores of the two groups are very significantly different, the scores being 2·48 and 1·55. Thus drinkers are about ⅓ SD more extraverted than non-drinkers.

SUMMARY

An investigation has been carried out to demonstrate the possibility of constructing short reliable personality questionnaires which might be of use in industrial and applied work and which could be administered in the usual interview situation.

An analytic sample of 1,600 adult subjects, equally divided as to age, sex and social class, was selected on a quota-sampling basis and administered a 12-item questionnaire. Six questions bearing on neuroticism and 6 questions bearing on extraversion had been selected from a previous item-analytic and factor-analytic study in order to cross-validate certain conclusions. Correlations were calculated between the 12 items and a factor analysis performed; this disclosed two orthogonal factors clearly identical with those of the previous analysis. Analysis of variance gave evidence of certain score differences due to sex, age and social class, although with the exception of the sex differences these were of minor importance. The 12-item questionnaire was found to have reasonable reliability and the two personality variables measured by it were found to be uncorrelated. The practical usefulness of instruments of this kind was discussed.

REFERENCES

1. Eysenck, H. J., *The Psychology of Politics.* London: Routledge & Kegan Paul, 1954.
2. ——, The questionnaire measurement of neuroticism and extraversion. *Riv. Psicol.*, **50,** 113–140, 1956.
3. ——, *The Dynamics of Anxiety and Hysteria.* London: Routledge & Kegan Paul, 1957.
4. Thurstone, L. L., *Multiple Factor Analysis.* Chicago: Univ. of Chicago Press, 1947.

Relation between Intelligence and Personality[1]

H. J. EYSENCK

First published in *Perceptual and Motor Skills*, **32**, 637–638, 1971.

THREE HUNDRED and ninety-eight trainee male nurses were administered two intelligence tests and a personality inventory. Nurses were found more extraverted and less neurotic than the general population. Intelligence was independent of extraversion and neuroticism but correlated negatively with the Lie scale.

The writer has argued that the personality dimensions of extraversion-introversion (E) and neuroticism (N) are independent of intelligence (Ref. 2), but there is in fact very little direct evidence on this point. The study here reported attempts to provide empirical data relevant to this issue. *S*s were 398 trainee male nurses, who were administered two intelligence tests and the PEN personality test. This test is as yet unpublished; it contains adaptations of the N (neuroticism), E (extraversion) and L (lying) scales of the EPI (Ref. 3), as well as a P (psychoticism) scale (Refs. 4 & 5). The intelligence tests were the Mill Hill Vocabulary and the Progressive Matrices (Ref. 8). The great majority of the nurses were between 18 and 30 years of age. The group was slightly above average in intelligence, but the means given by Raven are not age-corrected in a precise enough manner to make the calculation of significance values meaningful, and in any case the point is not important. The variances of the two tests were somewhat below the norms which have been accumulated in our department; again Raven does not provide the proper statistics to evaluate our results against his standardization data. On E and N the nurses do not differ greatly from our standardization groups; they are significantly more extraverted ($p < 0{\cdot}01$) and less neurotic ($p < 0{\cdot}01$) than the standardization group by t test, very much as expected (Ref. 1); they also have higher L scores ($p = 0{\cdot}01$) but do not differ on P. Table 1 gives these means.

[1] I am indebted to Mr R. G. S. Brown of the Department of Social Administration, Hull University, for allowing me to analyse the tests administered under his direction.

TABLE 1

MEANS ± STANDARD DEVIATIONS OF 398 NURSES AND 1,012 CONTROLS

Score	Nurses	Controls
Psychoticism	2·56 ± 2·36	2·50 ± 2·71
Extraversion	13·77 ± 3·41	12·75 ± 4·12
Neuroticism	6·79 ± 3·96	7·33 ± 4·37
Lying	5·76 ± 4·02	4·56 ± 2·95

The Pearsonian correlation between the two intelligence tests is 0·34, which is rather lower than usual. The correlation between E and N is —0·07, which is not significantly different from zero and supports the writer's contention that these two dimensions of personality are independent. The Mill Hill test correlates with E 0·01 and with N —0·05; Matrices correlate with E —0·04 and with N 0·00. None of these values are significant; the results thus clearly support the contention that temperament and intelligence are independent, at least for this sample.

Also included in the EPI is an L scale, assumed to test dissimulation or test-taking attitudes directed toward 'faking good'. This scale showed little evidence of lying by this sample, the mean value not departing from the standardization mean by more than 1/4 *SD*. In our experience scores on the L scale correlate negatively with intelligence, and the present study is no exception; *r*s for Mill Hill and Matrices respectively are —0·25 and —0·36. Also of interest is the correlation between L and N; Michaelis and Eysenck (Ref. 6) have shown that the size of this correlation varies monotonically with the degree of motivation to 'fake good'. In our case *r* is —0·26, suggesting a moderate degree of such motivation; correlations of —0·5 and above have been found in cases of strong motivation. This agrees with the slightly higher L scores of the nurses. P and L are only marginally related ($r = 0{\cdot}16$); E and L show an even lower value of —0·09.

As expected, the P scale correlated negatively with intelligence, the coefficients being —0·27 and —0·28. These figures are similar to unpublished values obtained in studies carried out on smaller samples in our laboratories. This finding may lend support to theories of 'mental slowness' in psychotic disorder, particularly schizophrenia (Ref. 7): it is from such findings that our expectation was derived. We may summarize these findings by saying that intelligence is not related to E or N but that persons having high L or P scores tend to have somewhat lower IQs.

REFERENCES

1. ELWOOD, R. H., The role of personality traits in selecting a career: the nurse and the college girl. *J. appl. Psychol.*, **11**, 199–201, 1927.
2. EYSENCK, H. J., *The Structure of Human Personality* (3rd ed.). London: Methuen, 1970.
3. —— & EYSENCK, S. B. G., *Eysenck Personality Inventory*. San Diego: Industrial & Educational Testing Service, 1964.
4. EYSENCK, S. B. G. & EYSENCK, H. J., The measurement of psychoticism: a study of factor stability and reliability. *Brit. J. soc. clin. Psychol.*, **7**, 286–294, 1968.
5. —— & —— Scores on three personality variables as a function of age, sex and social class. *Brit. J. soc. clin. Psychol.*, **8**, 69–76, 1969.
6. MICHAELIS, W. & EYSENCK, H. J., The determination of personality inventory factor patterns and intercorrelations by changes in real-life motivation. *J. genet. Psychol.*, **118**, 223–234, 1971.
7. PAYNE, R. W., Cognitive abnormalities. In H. J. Eysenck (Ed.), *Handbook of Abnormal Psychology*. New York: Basic Books, 127–131, 1960.
8. RAVEN, J. C., *Guide to Using the Mill Hill Vocabulary Scale and the Progressive Matrices Scale*. London: H. K. Lewis, 1958.

5

On the Unitary Nature of Extraversion

H. J. EYSENCK & SYBIL B. G. EYSENCK[1]

First published in *Acta Psychologica*, **26,** 383–390, 1967

STUDIES of extraversion-introversion as a dimension of personality have raised two difficult problems (Ref. 6): is extraversion a *unitary* dimension of personality, and are extraversion and neuroticism *independent* dimensions of personality? Carrigan reviewed the evidence and concluded (a) that 'unidimensionality of extraversion-introversion has not been conclusively demonstrated', and (b) that 'a clear-cut answer cannot be given' with respect to the independence of these two dimensions of personality (Ref. 1). In an earlier paper Eysenck & Eysenck have shown that one objection to the unitary nature of extraversion is not in fact tenable; sociability and impulsivity are not independent varieties of extraversion, but are significantly correlated with each other to form one supraordinate concept of extraversion (Ref. 10). This finding has since been duplicated by Sparrow & Ross (Ref. 12). The independence of E and N has been investigated in several large-scale factorial analyses, in which over 100 items previously found relevant to these two factors were intercorrelated and factor-analysed, for 600 men and 600 women separately; the method of rotation used was developed in our laboratory to permit analytic oblique rotation and extraction of higher-order factors (Ref. 11). Two higher orders factors, corresponding to E and N were found, and the angle between them did not deviate significantly from 90°, although the method of rotation did not prescribe independence of factors, but was determined entirely by the actual relationships obtaining within the data (Ref. 9). There is thus some evidence of both the unitary nature of extraversion, as well as of the independence of E and N. In this paper both problems will be taken up from a rather different point of view, which may throw some new light on this controversy.

Consider the conception of a factor as in some sense an underlying cause of the observed correlations (Ref. 5). The correlation of any given

[1] We are indebted to the Research Fund of the Maudsley and Bethlem Royal Hospitals for the support of this investigation.

test with that factor would then be an index of the degree to which that test measured that factor, i.e., its validity. If a criterion test could be found which correlated sufficiently highly with a given factor, i.e., which had sufficiently high validity as a measure of that factor, then it would be possible to use this test in a search for an answer to the two questions posed above. If the factor was unitary in nature, then the tests (or test items) constituting it should have correlations with the criterion which were *proportional* to their factor loadings, and if the factor was independent of another factor, then the criterion should not correlate significantly with any test (item) constituting this other factor.

The choice of the criterion test would of course be crucial in this argument. In the first place, the criterion should be chosen from a domain different from that from which the tests making up the factor were chosen. If the factor were determined by the intercorrelations between inventory items, then the criterion should not be an inventory item or a compound of inventory items. It could be a psychiatric diagnosis, as for instance in the studies using criterion analysis (Refs. 3 & 4), or it could be some objective behavioural test, or even some physiological reaction measure. Even more important is a second desideratum. The criterion should be chosen in such a way that it embodied a theory which predicted that it would be a good measure of one factor, but not of the other. Only by relating the criterion in some such way to explicit psychological (or physiological) theories about the nature of the factor in question can we hope to escape from the tautological arguments implicit in factor analysis.

The theory here chosen asserts that introversion is a product of cortical arousal, mediated by the reticular formation; introverts are habitually in a state of greater arousal than extraverts, and consequently they show lower sensory thresholds, and greater reactions to sensory stimulation. The theory in question has been discussed in great detail elsewhere (Ref. 7), as has the evidence regarding these and other deductions from it; on the whole the evidence, both physiological and psychological, appears to be in line with predictions made from the theory. The test used in the present investigation is the lemon test, so called because it measures the salivary reaction of subjects to the stimulus of having four drops of lemon juice placed upon the tongue for twenty seconds. The test was originally suggested by Corcoran, who has furnished data regarding its reliability and validity as a measure of extraversion (Ref. 2). The score on the test is the amount of salivation produced under lemon juice stimulating conditions, as compared with the amount of salivation produced under neutral conditions, i.e., when no lemon juice is present. Extreme extraverts show little or no increment in salivation, while extreme introverts show an increment of almost 1 gram; intermediate groups show intermediate amounts of increment. Eysenck & Eysenck have found a correlation of 0·71 on 50 male and 50 female Ss between increment scores and introversion, as measured by the EPI (Ref. 8); the correlation with N was effectively zero. No sex differences were observed.

The present analysis is concerned with results on the lemon test obtained from 45 men and 48 women, i.e. a total sample of 93 Ss; all these subjects formed part of the population of the above-mentioned study; 7 subjects were dropped because of failure to complete one question in the inventory. This inventory (the EPI Form A) contains 57 questions, of which 24 measure E, 24 measure N and the remainder constitute a Lie scale. The scores of the 93 Ss on the lemon test and the 57 questions of the EPI were intercorrelated, and the resulting 58×58 matrix of product-moment correlations factor-analysed by means of the principal components method, and rotated by means of the Promax Programme (Ref. 11). The first factor to emerge was clearly identified as extraversion, the second as neuroticism. Table 1 gives the items used, the scoring key (E, N, and L; when a minus sign follows the letter then the 'no' answer is scored positively), and the factor loadings for the first two factors. Item 58 is the increment score on the lemon test. It will be seen that the lemon test score has a loading of −0·74 on extraversion, and a completely insignificant one of 0·01 on neuroticism. The analysis was repeated for men and women separately; the factor loadings were −0·70 and −0·60 respectively on the E factor, and 0·02 and −0·06 on the N factor. Factor-analytically, then, the lemon test seems to be a pure (univocal) measure of introversion.

TABLE 1

1. Do you often long for excitement?	E	−0·48	0·33
2. Do you often need understanding friends to cheer you up?	N	−0·25	0·39
3. Are you usually carefree?	E	−0·36	−0·22
4. Do you find it very hard to take no for an answer?	N	−0·11	0·03
5. Do you stop and think things over before doing anything?	E−	0·40	−0·07
6. If you say you will do something do you always keep your promise, no matter how inconvenient it might be to do so?	L	0·07	−0·09

7. Does your mood often go up and down?	N	0·01	0·56
8. Do you generally do and say things quickly without stopping to think?	E	−0·57	0·12
9. Do you ever feel 'just miserable' for no good reason?	N	−0·02	0·49
10. Would you do almost anything for a dare?	E	−0·32	−0·05
11. Do you suddenly feel shy when you want to talk to an attractive stranger?	N	0·29	0·46
12. Once in a while do you lose your temper and get angry?	L−	0·22	0·19
13. Do you often do things on the spur of the moment?	E	−0·53	0·13
14. Do you often worry about things you should not have done or said?	N	0·17	0·61
15. Generally, do you prefer reading to meeting people?	E−	0·71	−0·02
16. Are your feelings rather easily hurt?	N	0·26	0·46
17. Do you like going out a lot?	E	−0·63	0·07
18. Do you occasionally have thoughts and ideas that you would not like other people to know about?	L−	0·09	0·28
19. Are you sometimes bubbling over with energy and sometimes very sluggish?	N	−0·17	0·57
20. Do you prefer to have few but special friends?	E−	0·40	0·06
21. Do you daydream a lot?	N	−0·05	0·66
22. When people shout at you, do you shout back?	E	−0·29	0·05
23. Are you often troubled about feelings of guilt?	N	−0·02	0·57
24. Are *all* your habits good and desirable ones?	L	−0·16	−0·00
25. Can you usually let yourself go and enjoy yourself a lot at a gay party?	E	−0·74	−0·00
26. Would you call yourself tense or 'highly-strung'?	N	0·08	0·07
27. Do other people think of you as being very lively?	E	−0·53	−0·27
28. After you have done something important, do you often come away feeling you could have done better?	N	0·20	0·50
29. Are you mostly quiet when you are with other people?	E−	0·62	0·21
30. Do you sometimes gossip?	L−	−0·07	0·07
31. Do ideas run through your head so that you cannot sleep?	N	−0·25	0·35
32. If there is something you want to know about, would you rather look it up in a book than talk to someone about it?	E−	0·54	−0·13
33. Do you get palpitations or thumping in your heart?	N	−0·20	0·35
34. Do you like the kind of work that you need to pay close attention to?	E−	0·22	0·01
35. Do you get attacks of shaking or trembling?	N	−0·25	0·50
36. Would you always declare everything at the Customs, even if you knew that you could never be found out?	L	0·12	0·13
37. Do you hate being with a crowd who play jokes on one another?	E−	0·49	−0·22
38. Are you an irritable person?	N	0·07	0·26

39. Do you like doing things in which you have to act quickly?	E	−0·39	−0·27
40. Do you worry about awful things that might happen?	N	−0·16	0·31
41. Are you slow and unhurried in the way you move?	E−	0·25	0·11
42. Have you ever been late for an appointment or work?	L−	−0·02	0·06
43. Do you have many nightmares?	N	−0·18	0·38
44. Do you like talking to people so much that you never miss a chance of talking to a stranger?	E	−0·25	0·02
45. Are you troubled by aches and pains?	N	−0·23	0·08
46. Would you be very unhappy if you could not see lots of people most of the time?	E	−0·40	−0·11
47. Would you call yourself a nervous person?	N	0·06	0·24
48. Of all the people you know, are there some whom you definitely do not like?	L−	0·07	0·04
49. Would you say that you were fairly self-confident?	E	−0·27	−0·51
50. Are you easily hurt when people find fault with you or your work?	N	0·35	0·36
51. Do you find it hard to really enjoy yourself at a lively party?	E−	0·65	−0·05
52. Are you troubled with feelings of inferiority?	N	0·01	0·73
53. Can you easily get some life into a rather dull party?	E	−0·48	−0·36
54. Do you sometimes talk about things you know nothing about?	L−	−0·08	0·20
55. Do you worry about your health?	N	0·04	−0·18
56. Do you like playing pranks on others?	E	−0·32	0·06
57. Do you suffer from sleeplessness?	N	−0·21	0·17
58. Lemon Test		−0·74	0·02

If, as pointed out above, the lemon test may be regarded as a relatively pure criterion test of E, then (1) its correlations with the individual items of the E scale should be proportional to the factor loadings of that scale, and (2) its correlations with the individual items of the N scale should be effectively zero. Such a test might have been carried out on the factor loadings obtained in this study, and given in Table 1; however, it might have been objected that such a comparison capitalizes on whatever non-relevant factors were present on the occasion of this experiment and might have influenced both the EPI responses of the Ss and their lemon test scores. Consequently we have chosen to use factor loadings obtained in a different and much larger study, using 500 Ss, half men, half women, who had been given the same items printed in Table 1, together with another 50 items (Ref. 9). This whole matrix of 107 × 107 items had been factor analysed in the same manner as the matrix discussed above, i.e., by means of the principal components method, followed by Promax rotation. In this manner the scales are weighted against our hypothesis;

not only are the factor loadings derived from a different population from that from which the item correlations with the lemon test are obtained, but in addition the factor analysis was carried out on a sample of items different from, and larger than, that used in our present experiment and factor analysis.

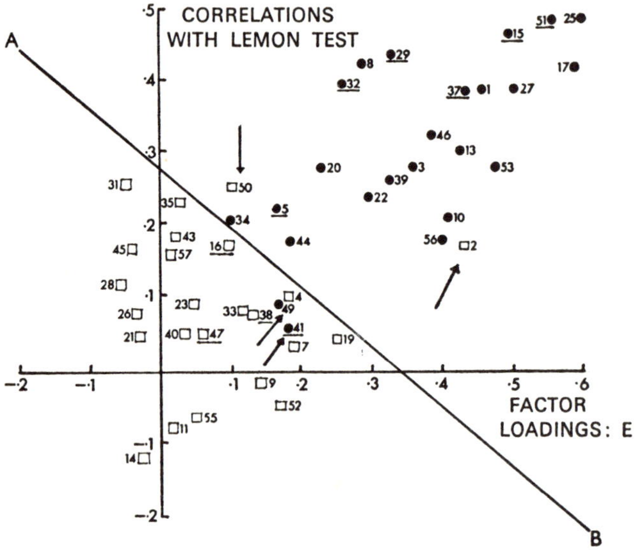

Figure 10. Factor loadings on extraversion (abscissa) and correlations with lemon test (ordinate) of neuroticism items (squares) and extraversion items (circles).

Results are shown in Fig. 10, where factor loadings have been plotted along the abscissa, the item correlations with the lemon test along the ordinate. Items constituting the E scale have been printed as dots, items constituting the N scale, as squares. L scale items, being irrelevant to this comparison, have been omitted in order not to confuse the picture. Items with negative loadings larger than 0·10 have been reversed in sign (multiplied by −1); these items have been indicated by underlining. It will be seen that practically all the E items have both high factor loadings on the extraversion factor and reasonable correlations with the lemon test, whereas N items have low loadings and low correlations. The line A-B has been drawn at the (arbitrary) level approximating a correlation value of 0·3, to divide the diagram into two parts; to the right (i.e., in quadrant 1) are the high loading—high correlation values; to the left are the low loading—low correlation values.[1] The former should be E items, the latter N items; it will be clear that in fact this is so. There are only two N items to the right of the line, and two E items to the left; arrows have been inserted to point to these four values. It will be seen that for all items (both E and N) having loadings of 0·20 or above, correlation with the lemon test are 0·15 or higher; at loadings below 0·15, only three are above 0·20. There is thus a remarkable correspondence between the two sets of values.

It is obvious to the eye that the correlation values are roughly proportional to the factor loadings for the E items; a correlation was made both with and without regard for signs. Both correlations are positive, with the former of course much larger; the actual values are 0·97 and 0·71. Both are sufficiently larger to allow us to say that the view that the items of the EPI extraversion scale measure a factor which is, as far as this experiment is concerned, unitary. This outcome is particularly reassuring in view of the fact that the criterion test used was chosen on the basis of quite specific theories regarding the psychological and physiological nature of extraversion and introversion; only by thus extending the circular arguments of broader coverage can we bring together the psychometric and experimental approaches.

SUMMARY

Scores of salivary reactivity to lemon juice were intercorrelated with 57 personality questionnaire items for 45 men and 48 women, and the matrix of correlations factor analysed. Two factors corresponding to extraversion and neuroticism were extracted; the lemon test score had a loading of −0·74 on the former, and of 0·02 on the latter, confirming theoretical predictions. It was also shown that questionnaire items having high loadings on E were also highly correlated with the lemon test score, while items having low loadings had low correlations. The implications of these findings were discussed for the unidimensional nature of extraversion, and for the independence of extraversion and neuroticism.

[1] The line is actually slanted towards the right because the average size of the factor loadings is greater than the average size of the correlations in the ratio of 6/5; in order to compensate for this, the intercepts of the line on abscissa and ordinate have been changed from 0·3 to be in roughly the same proportion.

REFERENCES

1. CARRIGAN, P. M., Extraversion-introversion as a dimension of personality: a reappraisal. *Psychol. Bull.*, **57**, 329–360, 1960.
2. CORCORAN, D. W. J., The relation between introversion and salivation. *Amer. J. Psychol.*, **77**, 298–300, 1964.
3. EYSENCK, H. J., Criterion analysis—an application of the hypothetico-deductive method to factor analysis. *Psychol. Rev.*, **57**, 38–53, 1950.
4. ——, Schizothymia-cyclothymia as a dimension of personality. *J. Pers.*, **20**, 345–384, 1952.
5. ——, The logical basis of factor analysis. *Amer. Psychologist*, **8**, 105–114, 1953.
6. ——, *The Structure of Human Personality*. London: Methuen, 1960.
7. ——, *The Biological Basis of Personality*. Springfield, Ill.: C. C. Thomas, 1967.
8. —— & EYSENCK, S. B. G., *The Eysenck Personality Inventory*. London: Univ. of London Press, 1965.
9. —— & ——, *Personality Structure and Measurement*. London: Routledge & Kegan Paul, 1967.
10. EYSENCK, S. B. G. & EYSENCK, H. J., On the dual nature of extraversion. *Brit. J. soc. clin. Psychol.*, **2**, 46–55, 1963.
11. HENDRICKSON, A. & WHITE, P. O., Promax: a quick method for rotation to oblique simple structure. *Brit. J. Stat. Psychol.*, **17**, 65–70, 1964.
12. SPARROW, N. H. & ROSS, J., The dual nature of extraversion: a replication. *Austral. J. Psychol.*, **16**, 214–218, 1964.

6

The Inheritance of Extraversion-Introversion

H. J. EYSENCK

First published in *Acta Psychologica*, **12**, 95–110, 1956

INTRODUCTION

THE DATA reported in this paper formed part of an investigation conducted under the writer's direction by Dr H. McLeod and Dr D. Blewett from 1951–1953. This investigation was in part made possible by a grant from the Eugenics Society. Some of the results have been reported in Ph.D. theses (Refs. 2 and 16) and in article form (Ref. 3).

The investigation as a whole was designed to answer a number of different questions, only some of which will be discussed in this paper. In essence we shall be concerned with two closely related problems. The first of these is the factorial definition and measurement of the personality dimension or continuum known as extraversion-introversion; the other is the discovery of the degree to which heredity plays a part in determining a person's position on this continuum. Most of the work on extraversion-introversion has been done with adult subjects; in this study we shall be concerned with school children, mostly of an age between 145 and 185 months.

A number of questions arose in the course of the investigation, or were from the outset considered to determine the design of the experiment. These additional questions, such as, for instance, the relationship between extraversion-introversion and Rorschach's concept of the extratensive/introvertive type of personality, will be discussed as they arise in the course of this paper.

THE PROBLEM OF MEASUREMENT

A considerable amount of experimental material relevant to the measurement of extraversion-introversion has been discussed in previous publications by the present writer (Refs. 5, 6 and 10). By and large the results reported there have shown that there is experimental evidence in favour of the existence of some such personality continuum as Jung postulated, at least among adults, that this dimension can be found, both among normal and among neurotic subjects, and that a variety of different tests could be constructed to measure this dimension with different degrees of reliability and validity. It was further found that, as Jung had postulated, extraverted neurotics tended to develop hysterical or psychopathic symptoms, whereas introverted neurotics tended to develop dysthymic symptoms, such as anxiety, reactive depression, or obsessional features. None of the studies carried out in this laboratory, or available in the literature, had concerned themselves with measurement of extraversion-introversion in children. Consequently it appeared worthwhile to test the hypothesis that behavioural relationships similar to those found among adults could also be found among children to define an extravert-introvert continuum.

Among the types of measures used with adults had been objective behaviour tests, ratings and self-ratings and it seemed desirable to include these divergent types of measures in the children's study also. In addition, however, it was decided to include a rather different type of test, namely, the Rorschach. Although the writer has been somewhat critical of its use as a 'global' measure of personality, some attempts made by members of the department had indicated that when scores on this test are used in the usual psychometric manner, meaningful relations can be established, although (or possibly because) the test thus loses its subjective and interpretive character (Ref. 4). The main reason for introducing the Rorschach into the experiment was, of course, the fact that Rorschach's theory contains the concept of the opposed types of the 'extratensive' and the 'introvertive' person. Although Rorschach workers often deny that these terms are co-extensive with Jung's typology, nevertheless it seemed a reasonable hypothesis to expect a considerable degree of similarity. Curiously enough no test of this hypothesis had ever been carried out previously to our knowledge and consequently a number of Rorschach scores were included in our battery.

In addition to the variables discussed so far, we also included a battery of intelligence tests and a battery of autonomic measures. There are two main reasons for the inclusion of the battery of intelligence tests. In the first place, some at least of the tests used for the measurement of extraversion were known to be also measures of intelligence. Without the inclusion of reliable and valid measures of intelligence, therefore, contamination between the effects of extraversion and those of intelligence might easily have taken place. This is particularly obvious in the case of some of the Rorschach variables. Thus, for instance, a high movement score on the Rorschach, according to Klopfer, indicates high intelligence. It also, however, indicates introversion. Assuming, for the moment, both these hypotheses to be true, before using the M per cent score as a measure of extraversion, we would have to partial out that part of the variance assignable to intelligence.

The second reason for including tests of intelligence in our battery was as follows. Most of the work on the inheritance of intelligence has made use of a single test. This does not seem permissible as Eysenck & Prell have argued in a recent paper (Ref. 11), because the fact that the score on a given test has a high h^2 when a comparison is made between the scores of identical and fraternal twins is indeterminate as long as we have no way of assigning the hereditary component indicated in this way to a specific part of the factor variance.[1] Thus, for example, if the Binet test were found to give much higher intra-class correlations for identical than for fraternal twins, we would still not know whether the hereditary influences thus indicated affected the general intellectual ability measured by the test, or the verbal ability also measured, or the numerical ability, or any of the other factors contributing to the total variance. The conclusion reached by Eysenck & Prell was that it is not test scores which should be submitted to such analysis but factor scores and accordingly a number of intelligence tests were included here to make possible such an analysis of factor scores (Ref. 11).

Also included were a number of autonomic measures, such as systolic and diastolic blood pressure, pulse rate in the resting state and under stress, sub-lingual and finger temperature, and dermographic latency. The main reason for the inclusion of these measures was as follows. In *The Structure of Human Personality* (Ref. 8) a number of studies have been summarized suggesting that autonomic lability may be related to neuroticism. If this were true, then it should follow that autonomic measures of this type should correlate with measures known to be good indicators of neuroticism, such as, for instance, body sway suggestibility. Thus, if autonomic measures and a few known tests of neuroticism were included, and if the theory were to be substantiated by our research, then we would expect, in addition to a factor of extraversion-introversion and a factor of intelligence, also to find a factor of neuroticism containing some, if not all, of these autonomic tests. In this way it was hoped to extend the work begun by Eysenck & Prell in 1951 (Ref. 11).

[1] h^2 is the symbol used by Holzinger to denote a statistic proposed by him as a measure of the degree of hereditary determination of a given trait or ability. For a critical discussion of it, cf. May (Ref. 17).

The actual tests and measures included in this study will be described briefly in the third section; a much longer description will be found in the theses by McLeod & Blewett (Refs. 16 and 2). In most cases the rationale for including a test has not been given here because considerations of space make this impracticable. A thorough documentation can be found in the writer's previous summaries of work done on these problems. Quite generally it may be said that a test was included as a possible measure of introversion-extraversion when it either had in the past been found in factorial analyses to have significant projections on this factor among adults, or when it had in the past been found to differentiate significantly between hysterics, the neurotic prototype of the extravert, and dysthymics, the neurotic prototype of the introvert. This would, of course, be reasonable only on the assumption that the behaviour of children and their responses to the test situation are similar to those of adults. This assumption appears to be reasonable and, as will be seen in the section on Results, is, in fact, borne out.

THE SAMPLE STUDIED

Little need be said here as in all essentials this study is a duplication of the Eysenck-Prell study. We have relied again on the differences found between identical and fraternal twins to give us evidence regarding the hereditary determination of any particular test score or factor score used in the investigation. The general theory is too well-known to be discussed in any detail; it depends on the fact that differences between identical twins must be due to environment; differences between fraternal twins may be due to either environment or heredity. If, therefore, differences between identical twins and differences between fraternal twins are equal in size, the total variance of the particular test under investigation can be ascribed to environmental influences. The greater the similarity of identical twins as compared with fraternal twins, the greater will be the amount of hereditary influence it is necessary to postulate. A convenient formula to assess the amount of hereditary influence has been given by Holzinger. His statistic, which he calls h^2, has frequently been criticized. A general discussion of the twin method, the difficulties which it gives rise to, and possible criticisms of it is given elsewhere (Ref. 11) and a discussion of Holzinger's h^2 statistic will be found in Ref. 17.

The exact details of the population of children used in the present study have been published by Blewett (Ref. 3). Here it is merely necessary to summarize the main points. Our sample was drawn from four metropolitan boroughs in South London. Our thanks here are due to the co-operation of the London County Council who wrote to headmasters of all the L.C.C. secondary schools in the boroughs of Camberwell, Southwark, Lambeth and Lewisham, requesting a report on any twins on their registers. 102 pairs of twins were located, of whom 56 pairs were subsequently tested. Four of these were later dropped on a random basis to equate numbers of pairs in the four groups: male identical, female identical, male fraternal, and female fraternal, retaining 13 pairs in each group. A thorough check was carried out to avoid various well-known sources of error in the selection of the sample; these are discussed in detail by Blewett.

The criteria used in this study were practically identical with those used by Eysenck & Prell, including rating scales for closeness of similarity of facial features, general habitus, hair colour and distribution, iris pigmentation, shape of ears, and teeth. Height and weight were measured and the ability of the subjects to taste phenyl-thio-carbamide was established. In addition, blood groupings and fingerprints were taken into account. Again, details are given by Blewett (Ref. 3) and there is little doubt that the final decision regarding the zygoticity of the twin pairs arrived at on the basis of all these criteria is essentially correct. The mean age of the children tested was 166 months, with a standard deviation of 11 months. Age was partialled out from the intercorrelations in the factor analysis as it seemed essential to have data not contaminated by this variable.

TESTS USED

The tests used in this investigation will now be briefly described. In connection with each will be given an index which will enable the reader to identify it in the factor analysis. The first two variables included in the factor analysis are zygoticity (index number 1) and sex (index number 2); these are not exactly tests in any sense of the word, but are referred to here, nevertheless, in order to keep all the index numbers together. The scoring in these cases was as follows: zygoticity $-M = 1$, $D = 2$; sex $-M = 1$, $F = 0$.

Next we have the set of intelligence tests included in this investigation. Most of these were taken from Thurstone's tests of primary mental abilities for ages 11–17. These are so widely used that it would serve no useful purpose to describe them in detail. The directions given in the Revised Manual (1949) were followed in the administration, and Thurstone's scoring methods were used throughout. The particular tests used were the verbal scale (index number 8), the numbers scale (index number 9), the space scale (index number 16), the reasoning scale (index number 17), the fluency scale (index number 18) and the total score (index number 19), calculated according to Thurstone's formula: $V+S+2N+2R+W$.

In addition, we used the Furneaux level and speed tests. These are described in some detail by Eysenck and by Blewett (Refs. 7 and 3).

Our next set of scores is derived from the Rorschach test. Standard methods of administration, enquiry, and testing the limits were employed. We followed the method outlined by Klopfer & Kelly (Ref. 15). The following scores were used: Popular responses (index number 28), average response time (index number 29), D (index number 31), To÷de (H+A÷Hd+Ad) (index number 32), FM÷M (index number 33), F per cent (index number 34), M per cent (index number 36), FM+m −Fc+c+C (index number 37), range of response times (index number 13) and lastly a composite score of pathological indicators devised by Blewett and given in detail in his thesis (index number 30). Most of these variables had odd and abnormal distributions and had to be transformed in various ways, usually by a logarithmic transformation.

Also included with the Rorschach group might be another test, the Rosenzweig Picture Frustration test, as this too is often considered as a projective technique. The only score used here was the extrapunitive one (index number 35).

The autonomic tests employed were as follows: Systolic blood pressure (index number 39) and diastolic blood pressure (index number 40). (Room temperature and humidity were measured at the time this and the other autonomic tests were administered, and wherever a significant relationship was found, temperature and humidity were partialled out.) The other measures used were pulse rate after stress (the stress consisted of pulling a hand dynamometer ten times, as hard as possible) and pulse rate after resting (index numbers 41 and 42). Sub-lingual temperature (index number 43) and finger temperature (index number 44) were also taken. Lastly, dermographic latency (index number 35) was determined using Wenger's method (Ref. 23).

The next set of variables consisted of ratings and sociometric measures. Questionnaire scales were used, both in the form of self-assessments and teachers' assessments. The scales used were adaptations of Guilford's C and R scales, which have been shown to be good measures of neuroticism and extraversion respectively (Ref. 8). The detailed scales employed are given in the theses by Blewett and McLeod respectively (Refs. 2 and 16). Based on these scales, then, we have a teacher's rating of extraversion (index number 4), a teacher's rating of neuroticism (index number 15), self-ratings of extraversion (index number 5) and self-ratings of neuroticism (index number 7). A lie scale based on the well-known MMPI—but adapted for use with children—was also employed (index number 6).

Two sociability scores were obtained, both derived from a sociometric examination. The subjects were asked simply to write down names of their choice to a series of questions. These questions were of the following kind: 'Whom would you like to sit by during class?', 'Who do you think would choose you to sit beside them in class?', 'Whom would you like to be with after school?' and so forth. The two scores were the total number of names given (index number 53) and the total number of different names given (index number 54). The hypothesis underlying this test was, of course, that extraverts, being more sociable, would give a larger number of names in both categories.

The last set of tests to be considered consists of objective behaviour tests. The first of these is the body sway test of suggestibility (index number 11); the second, the finger dexterity test (index number 14). Both these tests are described fully in *The Scientific Study of Personality* (Ref. 6). Next, we have three tests or rigidity taken from the work of Ferguson and his colleagues (Ref. 20). These are the opposites test (index number 22), the alphabet test (index number 23), and the arithmetic test (index number 24). These tests are based on the interfering effects of highly habituated culturally induced behaviour patterns in tasks involving largely cognitive processes. Another index of rigidity, called the index of flexibility, is a measure of the amount of change in level of aspiration by actual performance (index number 25). It is taken from a test using the so-called triple tester described in *The Scientific Study of Personality* (Ref. 6), as is the affective discrepancy score (index number 50) which is the sum of the goal discrepancy and the judgment discrepancy scores. The rationale and meaning of these scores are discussed in *Dimensions of Personality* (Ref. 5).

Two tests of persistence were included, namely, the leg persistence test (index number 26) and the dynamometer persistence test (index number 27). Both tests have been described in previous publications. As a test of expressive movement two of Mira's tasks were used, namely, the drawing of sagittal lines and the drawing of vertical lines (Ref. 19). The score on this test was the total area covered by the lines (index number 38). Two tests of humour were included, one of orectic (index number 46) and one of cognitive (index number 47) humour. The test consisted of 30 cartoons which had to be rated with respect to the amusement derived from them; the rationale for this test is given in *Dimensions of Personality* (Ref. 5).

The Porteus Maze test was also given to the children. As Hildebrand and Foulds have shown (Refs. 13 and 12), certain qualitative performances differentiate hysterics from dysthymics. Included in our study, therefore, were scores 'wrong directions' (index number 48) and 'lifted pencils' (index number 49). Two scores were also taken from the track tracer described in *Dimensions of Personality* (Ref. 5). One of these is an accuracy score, the other one a speed score (index number 51 and 52).

Last of all, a score was included consisting of the level-speed discrepancy on the Furneaux test (index number 21). Here a high score indicates a lack of such discrepancy; in view of results reported by Eysenck (Ref. 7), this may be regarded as evidence of normality.

RESULTS

Variables indexed in the section above were intercorrelated, the effect of age was partialled out from the intercorrelations and a factorial analysis undertaken of the resulting matrix. In order to avoid subjective determination of axis rotations by the writer, the rotations were carried out in the statistical section of the writer's department under the direction of Mr A. E. Maxwell. The results are therefore not influenced by the writer's own conceptions, although this may, of course, intrude in the interpretation of the results given later on. However, the reader will be able to check these interpretations against the figures. Table 1 gives the factor saturations for the 52 variables on the 6 factors extracted, as well as the communalities. The peculiar constitution of the sample, i.e. the fact that it is composed of closely related subjects, makes it impossible to apply any known tests of significance to the residuals and we have probably erred in taking out more factors than is warranted. However, no interpretation is here attempted of the last three factors and those with which we shall be concerned are indubitably both significant and meaningful.

The main loadings on factors I and II have been plotted in Fig. 14 and it will be seen that we are dealing essentially with the factors of intelligence and extraversion-introversion. The identification of the intelligence factor leaves very little room for doubt. The Thurstone total score has a loading of 0·947. All the other Thurstone scores have appropriately high loadings (verbal = 0·695; number = 0·569; space = 0·635; reasoning = 0·821; frequency = 0·629). The two Furneaux scores had loadings of 0·529 and 0·677. Finger dexterity, as is reasonable with children, has a loading of 0·389. Two of the rigidity tests have high loadings; the opposites test 0·579 and the alphabet test 0·656. The nature of the material used makes these high correlations intelligible and suggests that these tests cannot properly be used with children. It is not unexpected to find that the Mazes 'wrong direction' score has a high negative correlation with intelligence (—0·448) or that inaccuracy on the track tracer has a somewhat slighter negative correlation (—0·389). It may be surprising and is certainly interesting that the more intelligent apparently give more truthful self-ratings; the correlation between truthfulness on the lie scale and the intelligence factor is 0·374.

TABLE 1

Variable	I	II	III	IV	V	VI	h^2
22	0·579	—0·103	—0·055	0·091	0·019	—0·034	0·359
14	0·389	0·012	—0·215	0·037	0·099	—0·016	0·209
8	0·695	—0·016	0·014	—0·181	—0·050	0·062	0·523
11	0·258	0·090	0·061	—0·162	—0·062	—0·025	0·109
20	0·529	—0·006	—0·041	—0·293	—0·092	—0·042	0·378
16	0·635	0·105	—0·066	0·106	0·037	—0·033	0·432
19	0·947	0·075	0·124	0·036	—0·015	0·075	0·925
10	0·677	—0·019	0·291	0·285	0·101	—0·086	0·624
18	0·629	—0·071	0·225	—0·057	—0·048	0·092	0·465
9	0·569	0·096	0·200	0·047	0·025	0·162	0·402
40	0·232	—0·230	0·452	0·015	—0·014	—0·046	0·314
17	0·821	0·095	0·123	0·198	0·040	—0·021	0·739
23	0·656	0·151	0·264	0·197	—0·011	0·038	0·563
6	0·374	0·200	0·109	—0·301	—0·046	—0·015	0·285
34	—0·296	0·286	0·095	0·089	—0·124	—0·067	0·206
24	—0·161	—0·106	0·219	—0·140	—0·010	—0·099	0·115
48	—0·448	0·013	0·110	—0·231	—0·021	0·071	0·272
51	—0·389	0·162	0·041	—0·016	0·006	—0·098	0·189
15	—0·159	0·165	—0·177	0·084	0·021	0·005	0·091
44	0·031	0·300	—0·181	—0·066	0·056	—0·023	0·132
33	—0·090	0·501	—0·292	0·137	—0·013	—0·046	0·365
1	0·167	0·217	—0·166	—0·226	0·057	—0·010	0·157
46	—0·149	0·162	—0·026	—0·358	—0·077	—0·002	0·183
28	0·095	0·242	0·107	—0·227	0·023	0·106	0·142
31	0·164	0·510	0·106	—0·192	0·047	0·077	0·343
26	—0·004	0·229	0·129	—0·087	0·050	0·167	0·107
53	0·073	0·632	—0·017	0·061	0·011	—0·067	0·413
54	0·121	0·574	—0·094	0·094	0·029	—0·083	0·370
43	—0·121	0·200	0·620	0·034	0·011	0·096	0·450

TABLE 1 *continued*

Variable	I	II	III	IV	V	VI	h^2
36	0·191	−0·626	0·175	−0·084	−0·030	0·014	0·467
52	−0·098	−0·378	−0·047	−0·171	0·050	0·115	0·200
30	0·013	−0·396	−0·022	−0·272	0·096	−0·078	0·247
32	0·112	−0·189	−0·191	−0·264	−0·013	0·050	0·157
38	−0·045	0·027	0·184	−0·215	0·051	−0·087	0·088
49	−0·148	−0·111	0·177	−0·250	−0·092	−0·049	0·137
42	0·076	−0·066	0·913	0·148	0·006	−0·026	0·894
2	0·065	−0·057	0·855	0·122	−0·054	−0·025	0·781
29	−0·079	0·032	0·162	0·594	−0·126	−0·016	0·402
5	−0·104	−0·091	−0·282	−0·030	−0·135	0·011	0·118
27	−0·020	0·013	−0·197	0·141	−0·037	0·127	0·077
50	0·124	0·007	−0·447	0·123	−0·164	0·009	0·257
21	−0·136	−0·015	−0·240	−0·466	−0·172	0·035	0·324
45	0·193	−0·002	−0·216	−0·233	0·023	−0·049	0·141
47	−0·096	−0·056	−0·192	−0·406	0·001	−0·096	0·223
13	−0·006	−0·100	0·109	0·530	−0·118	−0·024	0·317
7	0·076	0·095	0·140	−0·350	−0·073	−0·023	0·163
4	0·042	0·176	−0·042	−0·326	0·073	−0·045	0·148
35	0·096	0·119	0·103	−0·228	0·021	0·024	0·087
25	0·032	−0·009	0·062	−0·197	−0·048	0·082	0·053
39	−0·019	−0·132	0·389	0·063	0·066	0·037	0·179
41	0·108	−0·123	0·839	0·115	−0·002	−0·013	0·744
37	0·065	−0·121	0·290	−0·059	−0·027	−0·011	0·107

An interesting feature of this study is the complete failure of the Rorschach scores to correlate with intelligence. The only one to achieve even the very modest correlation of −0·296 is the Rorschach F per cent. This, in spite of the fact that of all the scores included, the F per cent score is one of the few that is in general considered not to be a measure of intelligence. M, which is usually taken as a good index of intelligence, only achieves a correlation of 0·191. It is difficult not to conclude that the Rorschach scores which we have used here, and for many of which extravagant claims have been made as measures of ability, fail to measure intelligence to any significant extent.

We now come to the second factor which has been identified as extraversion. Before discussing this interpretation it will be necessary to present some details regarding the method followed in interpreting the Rorschach scores. While there is a good deal of agreement among Rorschach writers in the interpretation of certain scores, this agreement

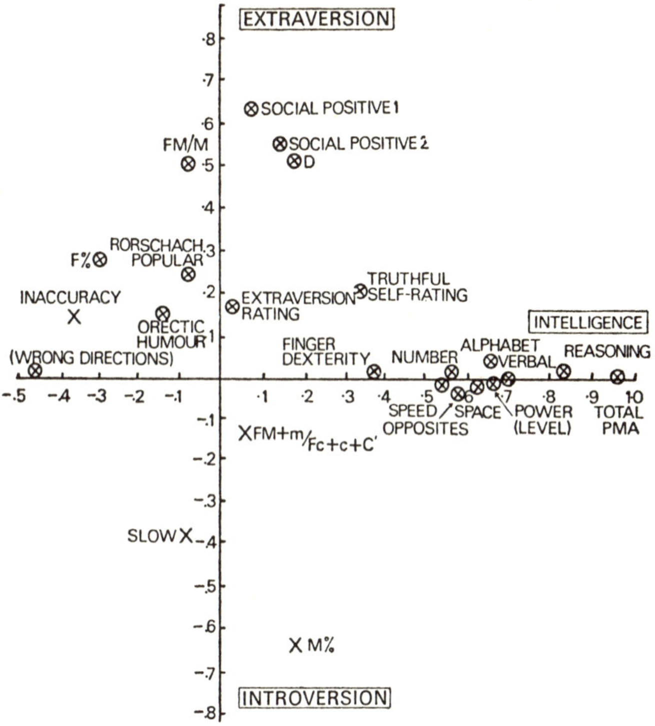

Figure 14

is far from perfect and it would be possible in a posteriori fashion to explain away discordant findings by referring to some obscure authority as having interpreted this particular score in the manner required to substantiate one's own hypothesis. To avoid this danger, the following method was followed. The scores used were communicated to an expert who had been using the Rorschach clinically and teaching it to students for a number of years. He was requested to write down in detail the relevance of each of the scores to the three variables of intelligence, extraversion-introversion, and neuroticism. He was to base himself entirely on the agreed interpretations of the most widely accepted Rorschach authorities, and on independent factual research evidence. His decisions were written down and implicitly followed in our interpretation; wherever necessary they will be quoted in full. This, of course, does not ensure that other Rorschach experts will necessarily agree; it does ensure that our interpretation of the results is not falsified by an attempt to justify observed findings in the manner outlined at the beginning of this paragraph.

Let us now look at the variables defining the two poles of the factor which we have identified as one of extraversion-introversion. The variable having the highest saturation on the introverted side is M per cent (−0·626). According to the expert, 'a high M suggests introversion, a low M extraversion'. This interpretation has found a good deal of factual support, such as, for instance, a recent study by Barron (Ref. 1) who has attempted to devise a psychometric measure of M by means of a series of specially constructed blots and who found considerable correlations between movement scores and introverted personality traits. The other introversion score is indicative of slow and accurate work on the track tracer (−0·378); this Himmelweit (Ref. 14) and Eysenck (Ref. 5) have found indicative of introversion.

On the extraverted side, the two scores having the highest saturations are the two sociometric scores indicative of social popularity and general social liking (0·632 and 0·574). This relationship between extraversion and positive social relationships is, of course, in line with our hypothesis. Only slightly less highly correlated with extraversion is the Rorschach D score (0·510). This is what our authority has to say about a high D score: 'A high D is said to indicate a "practical" man, a down to earth extravert; a low D is said to indicate a "theoretical" man, a "theorizer". A high D is associated with hysteria, a low D with dysthymia'. The interpretation is thus in accord with our hypothesis. Almost equally high as the D score is the FM÷M score (0·501). This score, of course, is not independent of the M score we have already considered, and can therefore not be used to add very much to our interpretation of the latter. However, for what it is worth, our authority summarizes the literature by saying that a high FM÷M ratio 'may indicate extraversion', a low FM÷M ratio 'may indicate normality, but also introversion and intelligence'.

The F per cent score has a correlation with the extraversion factor of 0·286. The interpretation of this score appears excessively difficult. Our authority says that 'a high F per cent is found in the records of psychopaths; a high F per cent is found in the records of many hysterics ("flat hysterics")'. This would suggest that a high F per cent is indicative of extraversion. Against this hypothesis speaks the fact that 'a high F per cent indicates "over-control" which could characterize an introverted neurotic'. Altogether, 'experts seem in some disagreement' so that we cannot really interpret this particular score. The next Rorschach score, the number of popular replies, has a factor of 0·242. According to our expert, 'a large number of popular responses suggests a dull extraverted person or hysteric'. Apparently 'a small number of popular responses suggests a person out of contact with his environment, or may be due to a perfectionist attitude exhibited by obsessive, compulsive neurotics'. In all, he concludes that 'a high number of popular responses might, therefore, suggest extraversion, a low number, introversion'.[1]

Three more scores are to be considered and lend weight to this interpretation. Inaccurate work on the track tracer has a loading of 0·162 which, although low, is in the right direction. Orectic humour also has a loading of 0·162 which is also low, but again in the right direction. Truthful self-ratings, with a loading of 0·200, is slightly higher and also in line with previous work which has shown a slight tendency for extraverts to obtain more truthful scores on the lie scale. With the possible exception of the F per cent score, we can therefore say that all the scores considered support the interpretation of this factor as one of extraversion-introversion.

A number of items have moderately high correlations with the factor but have not been considered in this connection because they neither argue for nor against our interpretation and may be chance projections on this factor. Among these scores are, for instance, item 44, high finger temperature, which has a correlation of 0·300, and item 40, high diastolic blood pressure, which has a correlation of −0·230. Our data are not sufficient to make it possible for us to say whether these additional items, which the reader may like to study intensively in Table 1, throw any additional light on either the identification of the factor or its measurement. The work of Theron and of Van der Merwe (Refs. 21 and 22), as summarized in *The Structure of Human Personality* (Ref. 8), has opened up the possibility that extraversion-introversion may be related to certain autonomic measures, and certainly this line of enquiry is promising and deserves to be followed up. It cannot, however, be

[1] Score 37, the Rorschach FM+m÷Fc+c+C has a loading of −0·121 and should therefore be a measure of introversion. According to our authority 'high FM+m is probably introverted, high Fc+c+C probably extraverted by majority opinion'. This is in line with our hypothesis, but the correlation is much too small to carry any weight. It may, however, serve to counterbalance item 32, the Rorschach To÷de where 'a high score is indicative of an uncritical attitude, perhaps suggesting abnormal extraversion'. Here also the correlation (−0·189) is too small to carry much weight. Ratios, in view of their well-known statistical unreliability, should never be used in work of this kind, particularly when the scores entering into the ratios are themselves not very reliable (Ref. 18).

maintained that at the present moment our results throw any further light on this problem.

A few words may be said about the third factor. This, quite clearly, is an autonomic one, having very high saturations indeed on pulse rate resting (0·913), pulse rate stressed (0·839), systolic and diastolic blood pressure (0·389 and 0·452) and on sub-lingual temperature (0·620). Finger temperature is rather out of line (—0·181), but this may be due to difficulties and inaccuracies of measurement. Dermographic latency has a relatively low loading of —0·216. The interpretation of this factor as an autonomic one appears somewhat invalidated, however, by the fact that item 2 (sex) has a very high loading of 0·855. This suggests that quite possibly the correlations observed are produced very largely by sex differences, and are therefore of less interest than they might otherwise be. No further analysis or discussion of this factor will be given here as it does not seem relevant to our main purpose. The same may be said of the remaining three factors, which do not lend themselves to any obvious interpretation and will therefore not be considered any further.

Factor scores were estimated for the first three factors. For the extraversion-introversion factors, the following items were used: 53, 54, 31, 33, 28, 4, 6, 46, 52, 36. For the intelligence factor, the following items were used: 17, 10, 16, 18, 8, 9, 20, 14, 48. For the autonomic factors, the following items were used: 39, 40, 41, 42, 43, 44, 45. Thus, each one of our subjects obtained scores on the three factors of intelligence, extraversion, and autonomic activity.

TABLE 2

	Intelligence	Extraversion	Autonomic
Intelligence	—	0·030	—0·103
Extraversion	0·155	—	—0·018
Autonomic	—0·074	0·001	—

Intercorrelations of factor scores for identical twins (below leading diagonal) and for fraternal twins (above leading diagonal).

Intercorrelations of factor scores were calculated for fraternal twins and identical twins separately, and are given in Table 2. It will be seen that there are no significant relationships between the factors. Next, intra-class correlations were run for the three factors between the identical and also between the fraternal sets of twins. These correlations, as well as the h^2 values calculated from them, are given in Table 3. A test was made of the significance of the differences between the intraclass correlations. For the intelligence factor, $t = 2{\cdot}13$; for the extraversion factor, $t = 2{\cdot}43$; for the autonomic factor, $t = 2{\cdot}09$. The t values for the intelligence and autonomic factors are significant at the 5 per cent level; the t value for extraversion is significant at the 2 per cent level. We may, therefore, conclude with some statistical justification that the differences observed between identical and fraternal twins are unlikely to have been caused by chance factors and would be found again if the study were duplicated. From this it may be concluded that heredity plays a significant part in the causation of all three factors.

TABLE 3

	Identical:	Fraternal:	h^2
Intelligence	0·820	0·376	0·712
Extraversion	0·499	−0·331	(0·624)
Autonomic	0·929	0·718	0·748

Intraclass correlations for identical and fraternal twins, on three factor scores.

One feature in Table 3 requires discussion. It will be seen that the intra-class correlation for the fraternal twins on the extraversion factor has a negative sign. This is an extremely unlikely occurrence on any reasonable hypothesis, but a thorough checking of the figures failed to reveal any errors in calculation. It seems likely that this value represents a chance deviation from a true correlation of zero, or of some slight positive value, an assumption strengthened by the fact that a correlation of the observed size is not statistically significant. Under the circumstances, however, we cannot regard the h^2 statistic derived for the factor of extraversion as having very much meaning, and it has therefore been put in brackets in Table 3 to indicate its extremely doubtful status. Much more reliance, fortunately, can be placed on the significance of the differences between identical and fraternal twins for this factor which, as has been shown above, is fully significant.

SUMMARY AND CONCLUSIONS

In this study an effort has been made to provide evidence for the existence of a factor of extraversion-introversion among children, similar to that found among adults and to measure this factor. By and large, this attempt has been successful and the factorial analysis reported in this paper gives clear evidence of a strong factor of extraversion-introversion.

It was hypothesized that the concept of extraversion-introversion, as operationally defined in the writer's previous work, would be closely parallel to Rorschach's concept of extratensive-introvertive personality. The inclusion of a number of R scores in the factor analysis made it possible to test this hypothesis and the results on the whole favoured acceptance of this theory.

Two further factors were isolated in the analysis, namely, one of intelligence and one of autonomic activity. These additional factors were found to be independent of each other and also to be independent of extraversion-introversion. Factor scores were calculated for all three factors for the members of the experimental populations.

As the major aim of the investigation was to study the effects of heredity on extraversion-introversion, the subjects of the investigation were 13 pairs of male identical twins, 13 pairs of female identical twins, 13 pairs of male fraternal twins, and 13 pairs of female fraternal twins. By using standard methods of intra-class correlation for different types of twins, it was shown that for all three factors, identical twins resembled each other significantly more closely than did fraternal twins. This was regarded as proof that heredity played an important part in the determination of intelligence, extraversion, and autonomic reactivity.

REFERENCES

1. BARRON, F., Threshold for the perception of human movement in inkblots. *J. consult. Psychol.*, **19,** 33-38, 1955.
2. BLEWETT, D. B., An Experimental Study of the Inheritance of Neuroticism and Intelligence. Unpublished Ph.D. thesis, University of London Library, 1953.
3. ——, An experimental study of the inheritance of intelligence. *J. ment. Sci.*, **100,** 922–933, 1954.
4. COX, S, M., A factorial study of the Rorschach response of normal and maladjusted boys. *J. genet. Psychol.*, **79,** 95–115, 1951.
5. EYSENCK, H. J., *Dimensions of Personality.* London: Routledge & Kegan Paul, 1947.
6. ——, *The Scientific Study of Personality.* London: Routledge & Kegan Paul, 1952.

7. ——, La rapidité du Fonctionnement mental comme Mesure de l'Anomalie mentale. *Rev. Psychol. Appl.*, **3**, 367–377, 1953.
8. ——, *The Structure of Human Personality*. London: Methuen, 1953.
9. ——, *The Psychology of Politics*. London: Routledge & Kegan Paul, 1954.
10. ——, A dynamic theory of anxiety and hysteria. *J. ment. Sci.*, **101**, 28–51, 1955.
11. —— & Prell, D. B., The inheritance of neuroticism: an experimental study. *J. ment. Sci.*, **97**, 441–465, 1951.
12. Foulds, G. A., Temperamental differences in maze performance. Part 1. characteristic differences among psychoneurotics. *Brit. J. Psychol.*, **42**, 209–218, 1951.
13. Hildebrand, H. P., A Factorial Study of Introversion-Extraversion by Means of Objective Tests. Unpublished Ph.D. Thesis, University of London Library, 1953.
14. Himmelweit, H. T., Speed and accuracy of work as related to temperament. *Brit. J. Psychol.*, **36**, 132–144, 1946.
15. Klopfer, B. & Kelly, D., *The Rorschach Technique*. London: Harrap, 1952.
16. McLeod, H., An Experimental Study of the Inheritance of Introversion-Extraversion. Unpublished Ph.D. Thesis, University of London Library, 1953.
17. May, J., Note on the assumption underlying Holzinger's h^2 statistic. *J. ment. Sci.*, **97**, 466–467, 1951.
18. Meadows, A. W., A Factorial Study of Projection Test Responses of Normal, Psychotic and Neurotic Subjects. Unpublished Ph.D. Thesis, University of London Library, 1951.
19. Mira, E., Myokinetic psychodiagnosis: a new technique of exploring the conative trends of personality. *Proc. R. Soc. Med.*, **33**, 9–30, 1940.
20. Oliver, J. A. & Ferguson, G. A., A factorial study of tests of rigidity. *Can. J. Psychol.*, **5**, 49–59, 1951.
21. Theron, P. A., Peripheral vasomotor reactions as indices of basic emotional tension and lability. *Psychosom. Med.*, **10**, 335–346, 1948.
22. Van Der Merwe, A. B., The diagnostic value of peripheral vasomotor reactions in the psychoneuroses. *Psychosom. Med.*, **10**, 347–354, 1948.
23. Wenger, M. A., Studies of autonomic balance in army air forces personnel. *Comp. Psychol. Monog.*, **19**, 1–111, 1948.

Part Two:
Extraversion and Social Behaviour

7

Personality and Social Attitudes

H. J. EYSENCK[1]

First published in
Journal of Social Psychology, **53**, 243–348, 1961

INTRODUCTION

IN *The Psychology of Politics* (Ref. 8) the writer put forward the hypothesis 'that "tough-mindedness" is a projection on to the field of social attitudes of the *extraverted* personality type, while "tender-mindedness" is a projection of the *introverted* personality type'. The personality dimension of extraversion-introversion referred to in this hypothesis had been given an operational definition in previous publications (Refs. 4, 6, 7 & 10). The social attitude continuum labelled tough-mindedness versus tender-mindedness had been discovered on the basis of factor-analytic studies (Refs. 2 & 3), and was found to be orthogonal to the radical-conservative continuum. A special scale for the measurement of the T factor was developed (Ref. 3) and was later improved by Melvin in a large scale investigation involving item analysis and factor analysis of a variety of different social attitude statements (Ref. 15); the final scale developed by him is given on pages 277 and 279 of *The Psychology of Politics*.

Two studies have been carried out to supply evidence regarding the hypothetical relationship between extraversion and tough-mindedness. In the first of these E. I. George applied the T scale as well as the Radicalism scale, the Allport-Vernon Study of Values scale and the Guilford questionnaires of personality factors S, T, D, C, and R to 500 middle-class male and female conservatives and socialists (Ref. 13). Using the R scale as a measure of extraversion and the S scale as a measure of introversion, a procedure which was justified by the empirical findings of Hildebrand (Ref. 14), he found correlations between R and tough-mindedness of between ·22 and ·56 for the various groups; for the S scale he found correlations ranging from —·03 to —·38. He also

[1] I am indebted to Attwood Statistics, Ltd., for permission to use data collected by them, and to Miss S. Kurlender for help with the analysis of the data.

carried out a factor analysis in which the R scale was found to have a loading of ·41 on the tough-mindedness factor; the S scale had a correlation of —·24. All these correlations were in the predicted direction.

Along rather different lines was the study by Coulter (Ref. 1), who applied the T scale as well as an abbreviated Thematic Apperception Test to groups of communist, fascist, and neutral subjects. She derived an extraversion score from the TAT and found correlations with tough-mindedness in all three groups, the correlations being ·301 for the communists, ·297 for the fascists, and ·307 for the neutral group.

While these two studies lend support to the hypothesis, it seemed desirable to submit it to yet another test in order to improve on certain features of the earlier studies. In the first place, the populations used by George and Coulter were far from being representative samples of the whole population; indeed, much of the interest of these two studies centred on the comparison of rather unusual groups, such as fascists and communists, with each other. The fact that the predicted results were achieved with all the divergent groups used in these studies must certainly be regarded as strong support for the hypothesis, but nevertheless it is obviously desirable to test the hypothesis on a somewhat less highly selected sample. In the second place the measures of extraversion used in these two studies were not specifically developed for the purpose, or validated sufficiently, so that the interpretation of the results is not quite rigorous. Since then a new measure of extraversion has been developed by the writer and appropriately standardized and validated (Refs. 9, 10, 11 & 12). It seemed desirable to apply this new E scale, as well as its companion measure, the neuroticism or N scale, to a random sample of the population who had also been given the T scale, in order to test the hypothesis in question still further.

METHOD

Subjects

A total of 944 subjects took part in the experiments. These were all members of a panel used by one of the major market research organizations in England for a variety of purposes; this panel had been selected in such a way as to be reasonably representative of the general population[1]. All members of the panel were sent the personality inventory,

[1] The original sample, as mailed, was selected randomly with substitution for refusals; the universe being individuals over the age of 15 living in private households.

which was filled in and returned; several months later they were sent the T scale—606 members of the panel returned usable copies of the scale, while 338 members of the panel failed to do so. (Of these 606, a few had not properly completed either the E or the N scale, so that not all comparisons and correlations could be run on the full number. The N involved did not, however, drop below 600 in any case).

Selection Bias

The first question that arises therefore is that of selection bias; in other words, it is possible that the more neurotic or more extraverted members of the panel might return more T scales, thus biasing the sample. The figures do not bear out this hypothesis; the mean neuroticism and extraversion scores of respondents are $22{\cdot}67 \pm 11{\cdot}19$ and $22{\cdot}74 \pm 9{\cdot}48$; those of non-respondents are $22{\cdot}57 \pm 10{\cdot}72$ and $23{\cdot}94 \pm 9{\cdot}38$. The differences between respondents and non-respondents are not statistically significant on either the neuroticism or the extraversion score; in addition, the scores are close to the population means as determined in the standardization sample (Ref. 12). We may conclude therefore that as far as the measures of personality features of respondents and non-respondents are concerned, they do not differ in any material respect and are unlikely to have biased the results of the study. It is still possible, of course, that the two groups might have differed along other personality dimensions, but as our experimental design calls for correlations with extraversion and neuroticism, it is the failure of the two groups to be differentiated in terms of these two variables that is important for our analysis.

RESULTS

For our total group of 606 subjects responding to the tender-mindedness questionnaire a correlation was obtained between tender-mindedness and extraversion of $-{\cdot}2479$. This is in the predicted direction and fully significant beyond the $P = {\cdot}01$ level. The result therefore bears out the studies previously quoted. There is also a correlation between tender-mindedness and neuroticism of ·2502; this also is fully significant statistically, but was not predicted. Speculation regarding the meaning of this relationship would probably be premature at the present stage of the research. A correlation was also run between tender-mindedness and age; this was completely non-significant, ($r = {\cdot}0104$), and it is clear that age differences need not concern us in our consideration of the relationships between personality and social attitudes.

The possibility has to be considered that the observed relationships might have been produced by class differences affecting both social attitudes and temperament. Accordingly the means and standard deviations of the neuroticism and extraversion scores were determined for the three social classes (1=Upper and upper middle class, 2=lower middle class, 3=working class) used by the organization concerned[1]. The mean neuroticism scores for Classes 1, 2, and 3 were 19·41, 21·77, and 23·51. With a mean standard deviation of 11·03 these means are not statistically significant. As regards extraversion the means for Classes 1, 2, and 3 are 24·10, 23·22, and 23·01; with the mean standard deviation of 9·46 these differences also are not significant. It may be noted that in a previous study with a short form of the personality inventory and a rather larger number of subjects (Ref. 11) it had also been found that there were no class differences in extraversion. For neuroticism a significant difference had been found in the sense that the lower-class group was more unstable emotionally by $\frac{1}{3}$ SD, i.e., by about the same amount as in this study. The failure of the difference to be significant here is presumably due to the smaller number of cases.

The question still remains as to whether tender-mindedness itself is related to social class. It is part of the writer's hypothesis that working class groups should be more tough-minded (Ref. 8) and some support has been found for this hypothesis (Ref. 5). To investigate this matter further means T scores were calculated for the members of Class 1, 2, and 3 respectively; these turned out to be 15·02, 15·55, and 14·09, with a mean standard deviation of 4·95. As predicted, the Class 3 mean is the lowest, and it is significantly lower than the Class 2 mean. Its differences from the Class 1 mean just fall short of statistical significance. Classes 1 and 2 are not significantly differentiated. The results therefore

[1] Examples of the kind of occupations which fall into each group are as follows: *Upper and Upper Middle Class:* All major professions such as surgeons, solicitors, architects, school masters at grammar and public schools, business owners, managers and senior executives and administrative grades in the Civil Service, bank managers, retired people formerly in this class.

Lower Middle Class: Owners and managers of small business firms, teachers at elementary schools, librarians, Civil Service clerical officers, bank or other senior clerks, supervisors and foremen supervising a substantial number of persons, master craftsmen with own small business.

Working Class: Toolmakers, engine drivers, bricklayers, fitters, lorry drivers, policemen, window cleaners, bus conductors, labourers, old age pensioners.

give support to the hypothesis, suggesting that in England at least the tough-mindedness attitude is found in the working class, rather than in the upper, upper middle, and lower middle class groups.

DISCUSSION

The results of this study on the whole are in line with previous work in supporting the hypothesis that tough-mindedness is linked with extraversion, and also that tough-mindedness (but not extraversion) is found more frequently among working-class groups. While both findings are significant, the relationships are not as clearly marked as one might have expected on the basis of the theory. There are several reasons why this may be so. In the first place the questionnaires used are far from perfectly reliable, and the observed correlations would undoubtedly be raised if a correction for attenuation were attempted. In the second place the questionnaires are far from being perfectly valid measures of the personality features they are assumed to measure. As the writer has pointed out elsewhere (Ref. 10), the proper measurement of a personality dimension such as extraversion would require objective performance tests, physiological measures, ratings and projective assessments, in addition to questionnaire answers; a single short questionnaire does not have a loading on a factor determined by all these measures of more than ·6 or thereabouts. It is clear, therefore, that considerable attenuation is introduced into the measurement of the relationship between the complex variables with which we are dealing by the limited validity of the measuring instruments. In the third place, while the hypothesis specifies the influence of certain personality and background factors on social attitudes, it does not maintain by any means that these are the *only* factors relevant. A highly complex resultant like a tough-minded or tender-minded attitude is obviously the product of a large number of different influences, none of which by itself could be expected to show very high correlations with the final attitude; it is the task of social psychology to tease out all the relevant influences and put them into a prediction formula in which extraversion and social class are only two terms.

SUMMARY

A random sample of the population constituting the panel of a market research organization filled in questionnaires of social attitudes and personality. Two hypotheses were tested, namely that *extraverts would have more tough-minded attitudes than introverts*, and that *working-class groups would have more tough-minded attitudes than middle-class groups.* Both hypotheses were supported by the results. It was also found that neuroticism correlated significantly with tender-mindedness; this finding had not been predicted, and no explanation for it is offered.

REFERENCES

1. Coulter, T. T., An Experimental and Statistical Study of the Relationship of Prejudice and Certain Personality Variables. Unpublished Ph.D. thesis, Univ. of London Library, 1953.
2. Eysenck, H. J., General social attitudes. *J. soc. Psychol.*, **19,** 207–227, 1944.
3. ——, Primary social attitudes: 1. The organization and measurement of social attitudes. *Int. J. Opin. & Attit. Res.*, **1,** 49–84, 1947.
4. ——, *Dimensions of Personality.* London: Routledge & Kegan Paul, 1947.
5. ——, Primary social attitudes as related to social class and political party. *Brit. J. Sociol.*, **2,** 198–209, 1951.
6. ——, *The Scientific Study of Personality.* London: Routledge & Kegan Paul, 1952.
7. ——, *The Structure of Human Personality.* London: Methuen, 1953.
8. ——, *Psychology of Politics.* London: Routledge & Kegan Paul, 1953.
9. ——, The questionnaire measurement of neuroticism and extraversion. *Riv. Psicol.*, **50,** 113–140, 1956.
10. ——, *The Dynamics of Anxiety and Hysteria.* London: Routledge & Kegan Paul, 1957.
11. ——, A short questionnaire for the measurement of two dimensions of personality. *J. appl. Psychol.*, **42,** 14–17, 1958.
12. ——, *Manual of the Maudsley Personality Inventory.* London: Univ. of London Press, 1959.
13. George, E. I., An Experimental Study of the Relation Between Personal Values, Social Attitudes and Personality Traits. Unpublished Ph.D. thesis, Univ. of London Library, 1954.
14. Hildebrand, H. P., A factorial study of introversion-extraversion. *Brit. J. Psychol.*, **49,** 1–11, 1958.
15. Melvin, D., An Experimental and Statistical Study of the Primary Social Attitudes. Unpublished Ph.D. thesis: Univ. of London Library, 1953.

8

Personality Patterns in Various Groups of Businessmen

H. J. EYSENCK

First published in *Occupational Psychology*, **41**, 249–50, 1967

COMPARATIVELY little is known about the personality of successful businessmen in this country, or about possible differences in personality between businessmen concentrating on different types of jobs. This paper reports on some data collected on 1,504 businessmen with the Eysenck Personality Inventory (Ref. 1), a questionnaire designed to measure extraversion, neuroticism and probability of faking (through a 'lie scale'). The respondents were on the files of a journal, *Careers Development*, which was sent to a large number of businessmen known to be successful; the sample was drawn on a random basis. In addition to being asked to fill in Form A of the E.P.I., each subject ticked one of 7 categories delineating different types of performance (personnel, finance, production, etc.) which he performed within the business in which he was employed. Of those who gave their ages, 334 were between 20 and 29, 665 between 30 and 39, 493 between 40 and 49 and 1 above 50; 18 did not give their ages. There was no relation between age and N or Lie score, by analysis of variance; for E the youngest group was significantly more extraverted than all the others, with a score of 11·22 as compared with 10·21.

The scores of the various groups tested, together with the numbers in each group, are given in Table 1; also given there are various comparison scores from the standardization data. Scores on the lie scale are slightly above those of the normal population, but not abnormally so; the data may be accepted as showing little evidence of faking. On N the scores of all the business groups are low; in fact they are the lowest scores returned by any group tested so far, including a professional group. The different types of position held in business by our 8 groups do not significantly differentiate them with respect to N, or with respect to the lie scale.

On the E scale the business groups are relatively introverted, but they are significantly ($p < \cdot 001$ by analysis of variance) different between themselves, with Finance, R. & D. and Consultants being the most introverted, and those who ticked more than one group being the most extraverted. Among the comparison groups taken from our standardization sample, salesmen are the ones most closely related to business; interestingly enough they come out as relatively extraverted, which is perhaps what one might have expected.

The results of this brief study indicate that successful businessmen are on the whole stable introverts; they are stable regardless of what type of work they do within business, but their degree of extraversion may be related to type of work. The data are probably reasonably reliable because relatively few respondents failed to answer, and because scores on the lie scale did not indicate any marked tendency to 'fake good'. The results suggest that the E.P.I. may have some modest role to play in furthering research into the personality patterns of persons engaged in business and industry.

TABLE 1

		Neuroticism		Extraversion		Lie Scale	
Group	N	Mean	S.D.	Mean	S.D.	Mean	S.D.
General Management	165	7·04	4·03	11·13	3·58	2·80	2·12
Production	135	6·90	3·77	11·05	3·72	3·08	1·69
Res. & Devel. tech.	574	7·42	4·05	9·98	3·88	2·76	1·49
Finance	132	7·53	4·49	10·12	3·40	2·93	1·97
Sales	168	7·04	3·64	11·33	3·98	2·93	1·52
Personnel	88	7·11	4·04	11·34	4·36	2·95	1·72
Consultancy	218	7·32	3·93	10·09	3·93	2·91	1·66
More than one of above	24	7·70	5·16	11·91	3·26	2·66	1·49
	1504						
Standardization Data							
Normal population	2000	9·06	4·78	12·07	4·37	—	—
Salesmen	37	8·38	4·72	13·63	3·76	—	—
Professional	23	7·95	5·11	11·40	4·91	—	—
Normal population	651	—	—	—	—	2·26	1·57

REFERENCE

1. Eysenck, H. J. & Eysenck, S. B. G., *The Eysenck Personality Inventory*. London: Univ. of London Press, 1965.

9

Personality and Sexual Adjustment[1]

H. J. EYSENCK

First published in *British Journal of Psychiatry*, **118**, 593–608, 1971

INTRODUCTION

In view of the considerable importance attached to sexual adjustment by many psychologists and psychiatrists, it is disappointing that very little work seems in fact to have been done in this field. There are, it is true, surveys of 'normal' sexual behaviour, such as those associated with Kinsey, but these are characterized on the whole by the serious limitation of using entirely descriptive statistics; these are useful in a limited sense, but are not very informative. The value of a mean of 2·34 for the number of times that members of a given sample indulge in intercourse during the week is doubtful when it is realized that some members of the sample have intercourse once or twice a year, while others have it several times a night; even if one could take the unaided recall of such events very seriously, and even if the rate for a given person were less fluctuating than it probably is, nevertheless when variances are as large as these means have little meaning or relevance. Clearly the important question centres on quite a different problem, namely that of personality traits and other factors giving rise to these very marked individual differences in sexual behaviour and adjustment. Kinsey and his followers have concentrated on the factors of social class and age, perhaps because these are relatively easy to ascertain; it is not so easy to ascertain the psychological factors involved, as many critics of Kinsey's work have pointed out. Nor have psychiatrists, in spite of their professional interest in this field, been more forthcoming; apart from isolated statements about the lower fertility of psychotics, the loss of libido in depression, its excess in manic states, and the widespread sexual troubles of neurotics, little serious and detailed work appears to have been done

[1] I am indebted to Miss Maureen Castle and Mr Maurice Yaffe for help in collecting the data here analysed.
The assistance of the Maudsley and Bethlem Royal Research Fund is acknowledged.

to relate personality traits, or even descriptive diagnostic labels, to specific types of sexual behaviour. Psychologists have been equally remiss; apart from a few undistinguished and not very meaningful studies reviewed by the writer (Ref. 3) little use has been made of the well-established research methodologies and psychometric tests available to them for use in such a situation.

The only apparent exceptions to this general rule are two studies both of which are based on the writer's general theory of personality description in terms of E (extraversion) and N (neuroticism); this theory enables us to make fairly specific deductions regarding behaviour and attitudes in the sexual field (Refs. 2 & 5). Both these studies (Refs. 3 & 10) make very similar deductions, and as these are also relevant to the study here to be described they may with advantage be summarized here in brief. As far as E is concerned, these deductions are based on the postulated greater cortical arousal of introverts, leading (*a*) to lower sensory thresholds and (*b*) to better and quicker formation of conditional responses; there is ample experimental support for these two points (Ref. 2). According to theory, extraverts, having higher sensory thresholds, would seek for stronger sensory stimulation ('sensation-seeking behaviour'); being less easy to condition, they would form the conditioned responses necessary for 'socialization' less readily, and would therefore be less likely to behave in a socially approved manner. The theory is of course much more complex than this but even in this brief statement will suffice to mediate the following predictions: 1. Extraverts will have intercourse *earlier* than introverts. 2. Extraverts will have intercourse *more frequently* than introverts. 3. Extraverts will have intercourse with *more different partners*. 4. Extraverts will have intercourse in *more diverse positions* than introverts. 5. Extraverts will indulge in more *varied* sexual behaviour outside intercourse. 6. Extraverts will indulge in longer pre-coital love play than introverts. These predictions are made with some confidence because they represent fairly direct deductions from psychological theory, based on large numbers of laboratory investigations of sensory thresholds, conditioning, alternation and other types of behaviour of introverts and extraverts; such predictions can of course still be disconfirmed, but at least the expectations are clear-cut and follow from theory.

With respect to N, predictions are less clear, and are therefore made with less confidence. On the whole one would perhaps expect high N scorers, who are theoretically characterized by a labile and overactive autonomic system, and are thus susceptible to fear and anxiety to a degree which may make them less likely to indulge in sexual behaviour, to worry about sex, to be disgusted by sex, and to have fewer contacts with sexual partners; this would be particularly true of unmarried subjects, because of the well-known difficulties in social relations of high N scorers (Ref. 5). There being no reason to assume that high N scorers would have less sexual drive than low N scorers, one might assume also that the reduction in direct outlets postulated above might lead to substitute outlets being adopted; masturbation, pornography and prostitution suggest themselves in this context. These predictions are more speculative than those concerned with E, and are not offered in any spirit of confidence, but they may be useful in outlining the field of study. The general predictions made are perhaps supported by the frequent observation of a direct connection between neurotic pathology and sexual difficulties, but in dealing with non-pathological samples such considerations may carry little weight.

A third general trait of personality has been investigated in the present study, namely the so-called 'psychoticism' dimension (P for short). This variable and its measurement have been discussed by H. J. Eysenck and S. B. G. Eysenck (Ref. 4), and by S. B. G. Eysenck and H. J. Eysenck (Refs. 7, 8 & 9); essentially this factor purports to describe the personality underlying psychoses of all types (approximating perhaps to some degree the 'psychotic triad' of the MMPI). Traits such as hostile, impersonal, cruel, play a large part in this factor; details of the items included in the questionnaire are given in the papers quoted above. Prediction is difficult, as very little is in fact known about this factor. The lack of personal involvement, the lack of human feeling, and the cruelty/hostility feelings which play such a large part in this factor suggest that normal sexual relations would not be likely to be associated with high P scoring, and that instead we might find relations reduced to a more starkly biological level. Again, it should be stressed that this is not a firm prediction, but a surmise based on the psychological content of the factor in question; disconfirmation of such speculative predictions would not be unexpected.

Giese and Schmidt (Ref. 10), using a very short scale for the measurement of E and N, administered questionnaires regarding their sexual conduct to over 6,000 German students, both male and female; most of these were unmarried. It would not of course be possible to quote in extenso the results of their study, which has been published in book form; some relevant facts are reproduced in Table 1. It will be seen that

TABLE 1

SEXUAL ACTIVITIES OF INTROVERTS (E_1), AMBIVERTS (E_2) AND EXTRAVERTS (E_3)
(From Giese and Schmidt (1968))

		Males (percents shown in italics)			Females	
	E_1	E_2	E_3	E_1	E_2	E_3
(1) Masturbation at present	*86*	*80*	*72*	*47*	*43*	*39*
(2) Petting: at 17	*16*	*28*	*40*	*15*	*19*	*24*
Petting: at 19	*31*	*48*	*56*	*30*	*44*	*47*
Petting: at present age	*57*	*72*	*78*	*62*	*71*	*76*
(3) Coitus: at 17	*5*	*13*	*21*	*4*	*4*	*8*
Coitus: at 19	*15*	*31*	*45*	*12*	*20*	*29*
Coitus: at present age	*47*	*70*	*77*	*42*	*57*	*71*
(4) Median frequency of coitus per month (sexually active students only)	3·0	3·7	5·5	3·1	4·5	7·5
(5) Number of coitus partners in last 12 months; unmarried students only: 1	*75*	*64*	*46*	*72*	*77*	*60*
2–3	*18*	*25*	*30*	*25*	*17*	*23*
4+	*7*	*12*	*25*	*4*	*6*	*17*
(6) Long pre-coital sex play	*21*	*25*	*28*	*21*	*16*	*18*
(7) Cunnilingus	*52*	*62*	*64*	*58*	*69*	*69*
(8) Fellatio	*53*	*60*	*69*	*53*	*59*	*61*
(9) More than 3 different coital positions	*10*	*16*	*26*	*12*	*18*	*13*
(10) Experience of orgasm nearly always	—	—	—	*17*	*32*	*29*

extraverts masturbate less, pet to orgasm more, have coitus more frequently, have coitus earlier, adopt more different positions in coitus, indulge in longer pre-coital love play, and practise fellatio and cunnilingus more frequently. It should be added that on some of these items differences are much greater for men than for women; this is expected on the grounds that in our society it is men who set the pace in sexual relationships, so that their personality is expressed more clearly in the procedures adopted. High N scorers (male) masturbate more frequently, have greater desire for coitus, and claim to have spontaneous erections more frequently; females have less frequent orgasm and stronger menstrual pains. No questions were asked regarding P, and consequently no results are available. (In this Table only unmarried students are included. Groups were subdivided according to their extraversion score into introverts (E_1), ambiverts (E_2) and extraverts (E_3). There were more men than women in this sample.)

Eysenck (Ref. 3), using a personality inventory measuring P, E and N, tested 423 male and 379 female unmarried university students with a 19-item scale of sexual behaviour, ranging from kissing to 'soixante-neuf'; factor analysis of this scale resulted in three meaningful factors identified as *petting*, *intercourse* and *perversion*. (The term 'perversion' is here used to refer to cunnilingus, fellatio, and unusual positions for sexual intercourse; this use is somewhat arbitrary, but is adopted for ease of reference.) N was correlated negatively with all three factors; high N scorers did less petting, had less intercourse and took less part in perverted practices. E was correlated positively with all three factors, but particularly factors 1 and 2; correlations with 3 were very small. P, on the other hand, had correlations with factor 3, and hardly at all with 1 and 2; in other words, perverted behaviour was related to P rather than to E. These correlations, in so far as comparisons can be made, are similar to those reported by Giese and Schmidt (Ref. 10), and bear out on the whole the set of predictions made on the basis of the writer's theory. It should be noted, however, that all the facts summarized so far deal with sexual *activities*, which are often circumscribed by external restrictions and opportunities; of equal interest would be possible differences in *attitudes* toward sex of persons differing in respect of E, N or P. It is the purpose of this paper to report such a study; predictions are of course similar to those already discussed.

DESIGN OF RESEARCH

The sample used in this research was the same as that described in connection with the previous study (Ref. 3); it consisted of 423 unmarried male students and 379 unmarried female students. These had been administered the P, E and N inventory and the 19-question sexual questionnaire mentioned above; details about administration and structure of sample are given in the previous paper. In addition all subjects filled in a Sexual Attitudes Inventory, consisting of almost 100 questions; this is reproduced as the appendix to this paper. A number of the questions were taken from, or adapted from, the Sex Inventory of Thorne (Ref. 13); others were specifically written to investigate certain theoretical expectations and predictions. Also given in the appendix are the overall percentages of 'Yes' answers of the male and female students to those questions, in so far as the questions can be answered by a simple 'Yes' or 'No'; these figures will be referred to again in connection with our discussion of sex differences. Several questions had to be changed in dealing with men and women; only the male set is given in the appendix. Question 76, for example, is re-worded in the passive sense for women: 'I get very excited when men touch my breasts'. These changes will be very obvious in each case, and do not require more detailed documentation.

Subjects were divided into groups for the purpose of analysis, taking each of the three personality dimensions in turn. Those high on a given factor are referred to as P+, or N+, or E+; those low on a given factor are referred to as P−, or N−, or E−. Subjects average on a given factor are referred to as P=, or N=, or E=. The numbers in these groups are as equal as possible, but as scores on the inventory scales rise by unit steps it was not always possible to prevent group sizes from becoming dissimilar. Table 2 shows the actual numbers in each group, for men and women separately.

TABLE 2

NUMBER OF SUBJECTS IN DIFFERENT GROUPS

	Male	Female
P +	110	87
P =	138	142
P −	175	150
Total	423	379
E +	125	121
E =	156	133
E −	142	125
Total	423	379
N +	139	116
N =	135	137
N −	149	126
Total	423	379

Most comparisons in this article will be made in terms of percentage 'yes' answers, and in view of the large number of these it would be impossible to give significance levels in each case. Table 3 gives the $S.E._p$ values for $N = 400$ and for $N = 120$, for different levels of p (p is the proportion of 'yes' answers, or the proportion of 'no' answers, whichever is the smaller). By and large, differences of 12 per cent will be significant for the N = 120 value, i.e., for comparisons between the personality groups, and differences of 6 per cent will be significant for the N = 400 values, i.e., for comparisons between the sexes; these values will be smaller for lower values of p. More important perhaps is the consideration that in each case where personality values are concerned there are three groups, so that if there is a monotonic relation this adds considerably to the significance of the observed differences. It would of course have been possible to have carried out analyses of variance for each comparison, but the results would have been prohibitively voluminous to print, and in any case only apply to single comparisons, not to large sets given below. Furthermore, we are concerned not so much with individual values but rather with groups of items measuring certain factors; congruence in these comparisons again validates conclusions which might not be significant for single questions.

TABLE 3

SIZE OF $S.E._p$ FOR DIFFERENT VALUES OF P AND N

P =	N = 400	N = 120
5%	1·0897	1·9896
10%	1·5	2·7386
15%	1·7854	3·2596
20%	2·0000	3·6515
25%	2·1651	3·9528
30%	2·2913	4·1833
35%	2·3848	4·3541
40%	2·4495	4·4721
45%	2·4875	4·5415
50%	2·5	4·5644

RESULTS

The relationships existing between the individual questions and the personality factors P, E and N are given in detail in Tables 4, 5 and 6. Each table lists, for men and women separately, the percentage of 'Yes' answers given to each question by high, average and low scorers on the P scale (Table 4), the E scale (Table 5) and the N scale (Table 6). In addition, each table lists the correlations between each question and the personality variable in question, again separately for men and women. These two ways of setting out the information are comple-

TABLE 4

PERCENTAGE OF 'YES' ANSWERS FOR P+, P= AND P− SCORES FOR 94 ITEMS OF INVENTORY; ALSO CORRELATIONS BETWEEN P AND EACH ITEM. DATA ARE GIVEN SEPARATELY FOR MEN AND WOMEN

	P_M			r_p	P_F			r_p
	+	=	−		+	=	−	
1.	35	36	42	−0·06	44	61	67	−0·17
2.	27	47	58	−0·17	64	85	85	−0·26
3.	21	15	25	−0·05	37	44	45	−0·14
4.	29	38	48	−0·13	53	58	65	−0·10
5.	11	18	18	−0·10	6	25	33	−0·30
6.	1	7	5	−0·06	3	15	16	−0·15
7.	51	49	43	0·09	49	48	36	+0·13
8.	5	6	9	−0·04	15	23	23	−0·11
9.	59	53	53	0·08	55	48	39	+0·09
10.	65	59	59	0·05	43	41	31	+0·07
11.	32	19	26	0·09	16	6	5	+0·22
12.	5	6	5	0·00	7	6	4	−0·01
13.	47	49	35	0·12	24	8	8	+0·22
14.	66	60	65	0·04	75	77	71	+0·04
15.	14	6	11	0·06	3	6	5	−0·06
16.	6	1	3	0·10	5	2	1	+0·08
17.	29	36	39	−0·08	41	39	43	−0·00
18.	13	14	11	0·01	21	18	29	−0·06
19.	12	14	8	0·06	16	18	15	−0·01
20.	55	51	45	0·07	28	27	23	+0·04
21.	38	43	46	−0·08	40	32	37	+0·01
22.	45	39	34	0·10	25	27	18	+0·07
23.	32	36	38	−0·01	25	29	23	+0·03
24.	2	2	2	−0·02	7	4	11	−0·03
25.	30	28	29	−0·02	40	43	40	−0·00
26.	73	69	63	0·10	92	70	64	+0·23
27.	20	14	13	0·10	22	9	11	+0·14
28.	36	25	25	0·11	26	14	16	+0·11
29.	22	17	19	0·01	33	27	21	+0·13
30.	17	15	15	0·02	18	6	7	+0·15
31.	67	68	76	−0·04	85	77	81	+0·03
32.	24	23	22	0·02	15	15	7	+0·04
33.	76	59	66	0·06	32	35	27	+0·10
34.	33	32	26	0·07	31	25	20	+0·09
35.	15	10	13	0·04	8	7	6	+0·10
36.	5	2	3	0·12	3	6	4	+0·04
37.	51	48	58	−0·12	48	49	46	−0·02
38.	95	96	93	0·03	100	96	97	+0·09
39.	90	86	89	−0·00	69	72	66	−0·01
40.	52	38	43	0·07	48	31	31	+0·15
41.	91	81	82	0·09	66	53	43	+0·19
42.	7	6	9	−0·02	6	25	27	−0·23
43.	68	51	61	0·04	30	30	21	+0·08
44.	11	19	23	−0·17	43	73	69	−0·29
45.	5	4	9	−0.08	13	37	35	−0·25
46.	32	22	22	0·14	7	2	3	+0·08
47.	61	62	60	0·02	15	8	5	+0·20
48.	21	16	17	−0·01	24	27	27	−0·02
49.	8	5	8	−0·03	11	15	12	−0·06
50.	35	34	29	0·08	32	27	23	+0·07
51.	27	20	27	−0·02	16	15	13	+0·05
52.	13	4	5	0·21	5	0	1	+0·22
53.	29	20	25	0·08	23	16	9	+0·18
54.	61	72	65	−0·00	80	76	83	−0·07
55.	5	1	1	0·10	5	2	3	+0·04
56.	15	9	12	−0·01	7	6	5	+0·06
57.	23	25	29	−0·05	22	21	27	−0·08
58.	25	20	26	−0·01	14	14	18	−0·04
59.	93	90	94	−0·03	86	78	74	+0·10
60.	30	17	21	0·05	16	13	11	+0·06
61.	85	82	85	0·03	78	62	61	+0·14
62.	7	10	15	−0·04	33	40	51	−0·12
63.	24	13	13	0·08	20	22	19	+0·06
64.	55	61	55	0·03	56	58	45	+0·03
65.	32	26	23	0·09	28	15	15	+0·13
66.	9	7	10	−0·03	8	4	13	−0·04
67.	37	34	31	0·07	29	25	18	+0·16
68.	91	87	88	0·01	79	65	55	+0·19
69.	8	3	3	0·08	20	20	24	−0·08
70.	62	42	34	0·25	10	8	5	+0·09
71.	56	55	46	0·11	44	42	42	+0·09
72.	75	68	64	0·10	55	·57	50	+0·04
73.	30	23	12	0·21	23	14	3	+0·18
74.	5	6	5	−0·06	6	11	9	−0·06
75.	79	67	75	0·01	59	59	51	+0·06
76.	58	52	61	−0·06	45	51	39	+0·03
77.	39	38	22	0·16	23	11	11	+0·17
78.	72	78	73	−0.02	74	70	68	+0·08
79.	82	75	65	0·18	53	34	26	+0·32
80.	43	45	27	0·20	60	42	27	+0·23
81.	62	63	63	0·02	21	8	5	+0·27
82.	39	45	41	0·01	11	8	7	+0·13
83.	49	36	40	0·12	16	13	9	+0.12
84.	69	58	53	0·18	41	30	28	+0·15
85.	58	64	64	−0·01	47	36	21	+0·24
86.	59	53	46	0·12	55	43	47	+0·07
87.	5	4	9	−0·02	3	14	17	−0·14
88.	33	33	31	−0·01	31	27	22	+0·00
89.	19	7	5	0·23	3	2	1	+0·12
90.	9	5	6	0·11	1	5	3	−0·06
91.	72	62	57	0·16	57	35	33	+0.22
92.	87	82	73	0·20	52	33	31	+0·20
93.	82	75	73	0·09	57	37	33	+0·25
94.	74	64	51	0·21	7	3	3	+0·18

mentary; the percentages show clearly whether the regressions are linear, a point assumed in calculating meaningful product-moment correlations, while the correlations give a single figure to indicate the strength of the observed relationship, as well as its direction. These three tables constitute the basic data of this study. In addition, a factor analysis was carried out on the intercorrelations between the items, for men and women separately; the fourteen factors which emerged will not be here discussed in detail, as this would take us beyond the confines of our concern with personality factors determining sexual adjustment; occasional mention will be made of these factors in our discussion when this seems helpful. The nature of the factors may be surmised from the labels given them.

The data given in Tables 4, 5 and 6 clearly require considerable effort to work through for the reader, and for his convenience an attempt has been made in this section to interpret these numerous figures and discuss their import. Inevitably, certain subjective elements will enter into such an interpretation, and the reader will wish to refer back to the primary data in order to make his own decisions about the accuracy and adequacy of the interpretation offered. Discussion will be arranged in such a way that each personality factor is taken in turn; brief mention will be made of the main factor loadings on the relevant sex factors, and then a summary will be given of the individual items loading significantly (above 0·1) on the personality factor in question.

The first personality factor to be discussed is P. This presents an interesting combination of promiscuity, pre-marital sex and curiosity with hostility and lack of satisfaction; the picture is of a 'lady killer' who has little love or kindness toward his victims, and who is on the whole dissatisfied with his sex life. None of the loadings of P on these sex factors are very large (0·3, with pre-marital sex, is the highest, followed by 0·25 for promiscuity), but they form a meaningful pattern, and show congruence for the two sexes.

The highest loading individual items refer to lack of concern with virginity (items 5 and 26), liking for impersonal sex (2 and 13), pre-marital sex (42 and 45), libertinism (44 and 79), liking for pornography (47, 81 and 84), liking for prostitution instead of marriage (85, 89), dislike of sexual censorship (91, 92, 93, 94), promiscuity (77), voyeurism (83), and strong sexual excitement (52, 3, 6, 7, 33, 37, 41, 46, 53, 82). These items indicate an intense preoccupation with sex in its biological aspect; other items indicate the morbid and indeed pathological aspect of the high P scorer's attitude. He considers himself deprived sexually

Table 5

Percentage of 'Yes' Answers for E+, E= and E− scores for 94 items of inventory; also correlations between E and each item. Data are given separately for men and women

	E_M				E_F					E_M				E_F			
	+	=	−	r_E	+	=	−	r_E		+	=	−	r_E	+	=	−	r_E
1.	31	38	45	−0·12	50	63	64	−0·15	48.	11	20	21	−0·11	29	25	26	0·00
2.	42	54	49	−0·08	77	86	78	−0·09	49.	7	7	7	0·02	10	16	13	−0·03
3.	17	23	22	−0·05	40	50	39	−0·07	50.	32	38	25	0·08	32	28	20	0·11
4.	42	42	37	−0·09	58	66	54	0·03	51.	10	22	41	−0·29	9	10	25	−0·27
5.	14	13	20	−0·04	21	23	27	−0·08	52.	6	4	8	−0·07	1	2	2	−0·07
6.	3	3	6	−0·03	8	14	16	−0·06	53.	20	31	20	0·03	12	14	18	−0·03
7.	45	49	42	0·03	54	44	33	0·18	54.	83	70	47	0·28	87	86	66	0·27
8.	6	7	8	−0·04	23	20	21	−0·01	55.	0	1	5	−0·15	3	2	4	−0·10
9.	63	55	46	0·13	56	45	38	0·15	56.	2	8	25	−0·34	1	4	12	−0·26
10.	58	60	64	−0·06	36	42	34	0·02	57.	15	27	35	−0·17	17	20	33	−0·13
11.	16	24	34	−0·18	8	4	12	−0·13	58.	17	23	30	−0·11	8	14	24	−0·24
12.	5	7	4	−0·00	5	4	8	−0·09	59.	96	96	86	0·11	86	80	70	0·21
13.	51	40	39	0·09	14	11	11	0·04	60.	14	21	30	−0·15	15	9	16	−0·05
14.	67	62	63	0·05	75	74	74	−0·01	61.	91	79	84	0·01	69	64	62	0·05
15.	7	6	17	−0·17	4	5	6	−0·18	62.	10	12	12	0·01	39	44	45	−0·03
16.	2	1	6	−0·07	1	2	4	−0·09	63.	8	19	19	−0·14	15	21	25	−0·09
17.	42	35	30	0·07	50	43	31	0·14	64.	62	58	53	0·07	64	46	48	0·14
18.	14	12	12	0·00	20	20	30	−0·12	65.	22	28	29	−0·03	13	15	26	−0·15
19.	7	9	16	−0·17	14	15	19	−0·11	66.	6	7	13	−0·15	3	5	16	−0·23
20.	40	47	62	−0·19	23	28	26	−0·05	67.	37	33	31	0·06	26	27	15	0·08
21.	48	40	42	0·00	31	40	37	−0·03	68.	91	93	81	0·13	71	62	60	0·10
22.	33	36	47	−0·11	17	20	32	−0·17	69.	2	4	7	−0.15	15	20	30	−0·20
23.	23	33	49	−0·27	12	18	46	−0·36	70.	52	44	37	0·14	13	5	3	0·06
24.	2	1	3	−0·01	4	10	7	−0·06	71.	54	54	47	0·02	47	45	35	0·08
25.	25	33	27	0·00	48	35	42	−0·00	72.	70	68	66	0·05	57	57	47	0·08
26.	77	65	62	0·06	80	71	68	0·16	73.	23	21	17	0·04	14	12	10	−0·02
27.	14	15	15	0·00	12	11	14	0·00	74.	6	4	6	−0·00	9	9	10	−0·09
28.	22	28	33	−0·08	14	15	24	−0·15	75.	70	74	77	−0·05	60	58	49	0·11
29.	17	19	22	−0·05	30	28	20	0·08	76.	55	58	58	−0·04	51	44	40	0·07
30.	15	15	18	−0·03	11	5	12	−0·04	77.	48	30	19	0·22	19	11	12	0·09
31.	84	76	54	0·29	93	86	62	0·40	78.	71	76	75	−0·04	72	71	67	0·02
32.	13	23	31	−0·18	12	11	14	−0·05	79.	76	71	72	0·03	41	34	30	0·14
33.	71	64	65	0·05	37	32	25	0·12	80.	34	37	40	−0·04	50	35	35	0·04
34.	23	28	37	−0·09	22	23	29	−0·07	81.	58	65	65	−0·03	10	10	9	0·00
35.	3	13	19	−0·19	6	5	10	−0·12	82.	40	42	43	−0·01	12	8	6	0·12
36.	2	2	7	−0·12	3	7	3	−0·02	83.	42	33	49	−0·04	11	14	10	−0·02
37.	50	52	56	−0·07	43	54	45	−0·07	84.	66	58	52	0·11	33	34	29	0·07
38.	93	96	94	−0·03	98	95	98	0·01	85.	68	66	54	0·12	38	31	29	0·09
39.	90	85	89	0·02	76	67	64	0·12	86.	59	49	48	0·05	51	50	40	0·09
40.	42	46	43	−0·05	37	38	29	0·08	87.	3	6	9	−0·09	14	11	14	−0·07
41.	87	82	83	0·01	58	53	45	0·16	88.	34	30	32	0·01	25	32	20	0·04
42.	6	8	8	−0·09	15	22	27	−0·13	89.	10	10	8	0·07	4	1	2	0·04
43.	57	60	63	−0·03	32	28	20	0·18	90.	5	6	9	−0.02	6	3	2	0·01
44.	11	20	23	−0·19	53	70	70	−0·19	91.	73	59	58	0.08	44	38	36	0·10
45.	3	4	11	−0·14	21	35	35	−0·14	92.	88	79	73	0·14	41	32	38	0·06
46.	28	26	20	0·13	5	2	4	0·03	93.	82	78	68	0·15	41	41	38	0·06
47.	56	63	62	0·00	8	7	10	−0·04	94.	75	63	47	0·21	6	3	2	0·09

(11) and dissatisfied with his sex life (4, 22), in spite of the fact that he has had more sexual experience than the low P scorer; he feels hostility to his sex partner (73, 80), is troubled by perverted thoughts (28, 29), and has homosexual leanings (16, 30, 36, 40). Taking one's pleasures where one finds them (70) has clearly not brought him much happiness; the libertinism is marred by a pathological streak which may justify the clinical connotations of the 'P' label.

The high E scorer is also characterized by the promiscuity factor, but in him it is allied most prominently with lack of nervousness and with satisfaction. The highest loadings are with lack of nervousness (0·35) and with promiscuity (0·27); here apparently we have a happy philanderer, who derives satisfaction from his sexual behaviour. The individual items having the highest loadings emphasize the extravert's social facility with the opposite sex (23, 31, 56, 51, 54, 58, 66, 17), his liking for sexual activity (59, 69, 9, 18, 19, 32, 41, 55), his contentment with his sexual life (11, 15, 20, 22) and his lack of worry about it (60, 63). He too is easily excited sexually, (7, 33, 39, 43, 46) and endorses pre-marital sex (26, 42, 45); he too is promiscuous (77, 44), but he lacks the pathological element of the high P scorer (28, 35), and his liking for pornography is very slight (84, 85, 91, 92, 93, 94). Homosexuality (36) is no problem to him, and offers no attraction.

High N scorers show a different combination of excitement and approval for pre-marital sex with the other factors: they are characterized by low satisfaction and high guilt feelings. Loadings are highest on guilt (0·30), and lack of satisfaction (0·25); excitement loads more highly for the men (0·20). Individual items emphasize the same features; particularly prominent are the lack of satisfaction derived from sex (4, 20, 22), the guilt feelings associated with a strong conscience (48, 25), the worry about sexual activities (60, 63), the problem of controlling sexual thoughts (35, 7, 28, 29), and the fears and difficulties associated with contacts with the opposite sex (56, 17, 54, 56, 31). Blame is attached to the inhibiting influence of the parents (34), religion (49) and 'bad experiences' (27). Sexual behaviour is seen as both troublesome (21, 19, 66) and disgusting (11), and the high N scorer stresses his inability to contact members of the other sex (15, 23); in spite of all this he has strong sexual drives (33, 41, 43, 50, 52) which he finds it difficult to control (32, 53). Homosexuality is a problem (16, 36, 40). There is some evidence of liking for pornography (83, 85, 93, 94), but much less so than in the high P scorer; it almost seems a substitute for the unattainable sexual contacts with real life partners. Lastly, there is a

Table 6

Percentage of 'Yes' Answers for N+, N= and N− scores for 94 items of inventory; also correlations between N and each item. Data are given separately for men and women

	N_M				N_F			
	+	=	−	r_N	+	=	−	r_N
1.	43	36	36	0·10	60	61	56	0·03
2.	50	50	46	0·07	79	82	79	−0·05
3.	28	19	16	0·11	47	44	39	0·06
4.	25	41	53	−0·27	49	53	77	−0·30
5.	17	19	13	0·01	20	28	22	−0·05
6.	3	4	6	−0·12	6	15	16	−0·17
7.	57	47	34	0·25	53	37	42	0·12
8.	8	7	5	0·05	25	20	20	−0·02
9.	59	58	48	0·07	48	44	47	0·02
10.	64	61	57	0·09	42	39	31	0·14
11.	37	22	16	0·25	13	9	2	0·20
12.	5	6	5	0·04	8	7	2	0·09
13.	45	44	41	0.02	11	13	11	0·00
14.	64	61	66	−0·07	71	73	79	−0·05
15.	18	5	7	0·15	8	4	3	0·10
16.	6	2	1	0·11	4	2	1	0·05
17.	28	36	42	−0·16	25	45	52	−0·24
18.	14	16	7	0·08	25	26	18	0·07
19.	14	10	8	0·11	24	15	10	0·15
20.	70	47	34	0·31	35	29	13	0·24
21.	39	41	49	−0·08	30	36	41	−0·13
22.	53	37	26	0·29	34	26	10	0·28
23.	42	36	30	0·12	27	28	22	0·04
24.	4	1	1	0·09	9	7	6	0·04
25.	38	32	17	0·20	55	39	30	0·23
26.	59	66	77	−0·11	79	73	67	0·11
27.	22	11	11	0·16	19	10	10	0·11
28.	40	29	15	0·25	29	15	10	0·21
29.	29	20	9	0·24	35	27	16	0·23
30.	23	14	10	0·17	14	7	7	0·09
31.	64	73	76	−0·12	79	77	85	−0·05
32.	35	22	11	0.26	23	7	6	0·19
33.	73	64	62	0·14	38	27	29	0·03
34.	39	33	18	0·18	39	22	14	0·27
35.	24	11	2	0·33	12	7	2	0·18
36.	6	2	2	0·14	6	4	3	0·05
37.	55	49	54	0·04	49	48	45	0·02
38.	95	95	94	0·01	97	96	98	0.02
39.	91	88	85	0·08	60	71	75	−0·15
40.	48	41	41	0·11	41	35	29	0·08
41.	90	85	77	0·18	56	50	49	0·05
42.	7	9	6	0·01	15	27	21	−0·07
43.	65	61	54	0·15	34	23	24	0·05
44.	19	21	15	0·05	72	61	63	0·04
45.	8	7	4	0·07	28	34	29	−0·03
46.	27	21	24	0·04	4	2	4	0·01
47.	65	64	54	0·08	13	7	5	0·13

	N_M				N_F			
	+	=	−	r_N	+	=	−	r_N
48.	30	17	7	0·27	48	21	12	0·33
49.	9	9	3	0·14	16	13	10	0·03
50.	42	30	26	0·18	34	25	22	0·14
51.	41	16	17	0·30	23	15	6	0·21
52.	14	2	2	0·27	3	1	0	0·08
53.	33	24	16	0·16	23	15	7	0·19
54.	53	68	77	−0·21	72	80	87	−0·14
55.	4	1	0	0·18	4	3	2	0·04
56.	20	7	9	0·22	8	6	3	0·11
57.	35	23	20	0·15	34	23	13	0·15
58.	32	22	17	0·23	22	15	10	0·11
59.	88	95	94	−0·07	78	77	80	0·02
60.	44	16	7	0·42	28	11	2	0·32
61.	81	84	87	−0·07	66	66	63	0·09
62.	9	13	13	−0·08	44	43	41	−0·06
63.	30	11	6	0·34	39	15	9	0·33
64.	60	59	52	0·06	53	53	52	−0·02
65.	36	27	17	0·19	29	16	10	0·20
66.	16	4	6	0·18	10	9	5	0·05
67.	30	39	32	0·01	30	20	20	0·06
68.	85	90	91	−0·10	72	60	63	0·05
69.	6	4	3	0·08	27	19	20	0·04
70.	47	42	43	0·05	8	7	7	−0·05
71.	53	53	49	0·02	45	42	40	0·03
72.	74	63	67	0·03	60	49	53	0·05
73.	25	21	15	0·18	16	15	5	0·12
74.	4	7	4	0·09	9	9	10	−0·03
75.	77	71	73	0·06	57	55	55	0·02
76.	54	63	55	0·05	52	44	40	0·05
77.	35	33	29	0·02	14	16	12	0·02
78.	75	72	76	−0·01	72	72	67	0·05
79.	71	71	76	−0·06	41	36	28	0·12
80.	50	36	26	0·21	53	39	29	0·18
81.	65	67	57	0·10	12	9	8	0·05
82.	47	46	33	0·16	11	7	8	0·09
83.	50	41	33	0·14	16	9	11	0·07
84.	60	56	60	0·01	36	31	29	0·06
85.	63	61	63	−0·01	41	28	29	0·12
86.	53	49	52	0·02	58	46	39	0·10
87.	11	4	3	0·11	9	16	13	−0·06
88.	33	32	30	0·02	28	24	26	−0·04
89.	9	8	10	0·05	2	2	2	0·01
90.	10	4	5	0·09	3	5	2	0·01
91.	68	62	59	0·05	45	37	36	0·08
92.	83	79	77	0·09	41	36	33	0·02
93.	77	76	75	0·00	49	38	34	0·10
94.	61	59	64	0·05	3	4	4	0·10

tendency to be hostile to the sex partner (80, 73), but again the context suggests a different interpretation to the hostility of the high P scorer; here the hostility may spring from the failure to acquire a sex partner in the first place!

Taking an overall view, one might say that, as expected, high P and N scorers show a distinctly pathological pattern of sexual reactions. Both are characterized by strong sexual drives (the former less so than the latter), but whereas the high P scorer 'acts out' his libidinous, promiscuous and perverse desires, the high N scorer does not; instead he is beset by a whole set of inhibitions, worries, and guilt feelings which effectively prevent him from consummating his desires. Yet both groups are dissatisfied with their patterns of sexual performance, although presumably for different reasons; this dissatisfaction constitutes the strongest evidence for the hypothesis that both are to some degree 'pathological'. (It would clearly not be adequate to justify this term on the grounds of either statistical infrequency of occurrence, or of moral and ethical undesirability of the conduct in question; it is because both groups are so dissatisfied with their behaviour that one may justly infer that it is not appropriate.) Both groups are similar in that they view their sex partners with some hostility, like pornography, and have homosexual leanings; yet as already pointed out, the different setting in which these items occur suggests different interpretations of the motivation involved, at least for the first two points.

As regards the E factor, the evidence would seem to suggest that here we have two non-pathological ways of sexual adjustment, the extraverted and the introverted, which are opposed in a very meaningful manner. The extravert endorses the 'permissive', promiscuous approach to sex, with frequent change of sex partner and much 'healthy appetite' for frequent sexual contacts. The introvert endorses the orthodox Christian approach with fidelity, stress on virginity, and less purely biological factors as the prime contents. Taken to their extremes, these approaches become the 'libertine' and the 'puritan' respectively, but if not taken to excess they are probably both viable modes of adjustment. The extravert seems more satisfied with his way of life, and is of course better able to contact members of the opposite sex, but this may be an artefact of the particular sample taken; at 20, unmarried youngsters quite naturally have some difficulties in living up to introverted ideals. At 40, the happily married introvert may show better adjustment than the extravert suffering from the 'seven year itch'. This is of course merely speculation, but it may serve to emphasize the restrictions imposed on interpretation by the specific nature of the sample studied.[1]

Having thus briefly discussed the sexual attitudes associated with P, E and N, it may be worth while to devote a few sentences to a discussion of the observed differences between male and female attitudes, as set out in numerical form in the Appendix. (In assessing percentage differences, it is of course essential to bear in mind the different S.E.s at different levels of p, as set out in Table 3.) Overwhelmingly outstanding among items giving marked differences between the sexes are items relating to pornography (47, 81, 84, 91, 92, 93), orgies (44, 94), voyeurism (83, 62) and prostitution (85), closely followed by impersonal sex (2, 13). Sexual excitement is close behind (33, 41, 43, 46, 82, 3, 39); in all this of course males have higher rates of endorsement than females. Premarital sex is also favoured more by the males (45, 70, 79, 42), as is promiscuity (77). But contentment in their sex life is more marked

[1] The data presented in Tables 4, 5 and 6 enable us to say something about the consistency of the personality-attitude relations between sexes, and also about the similarity or dissimilarity of attitudes held by different personality types. Given in these tables are six columns (r_P, r_E and r_N, each replicated for males and females) which report the correlations of each of the 94 items with P, E and N. These six columns were themselves correlated, in the hope that the results would throw some light on the two problems mentioned above. First consider the male-female correlations within personality type, i.e., P_M vs. $P_F = 0{\cdot}69$; E_M vs. $E_F = 0{\cdot}80$; N_M vs. $N_F = 0{\cdot}77$. These demonstrate that personality scale–attitude item correlations which are high for one sex are also high for the other; there is clearly a considerable amount of consistency here, particularly for the E scale, slightly less so for the N scale, and least of all for the P scale. This is not unexpected, as the P scale is the least reliable and has had much less experimental work associated with it than the other two scales. When we turn from these intra-scale correlations to inter-scale correlations, we find results which may be set out in the form of a small table:

	P × E	P × N	E × N
Male vs. male: ...	0·28	0·23	−0·61
Female vs. female: ...	0·39	0·38	−0·25
Male vs. female: ...	0·22	0·33	−0·39
Female vs. male: ...	0·32	0·14	−0·44

Clearly the sexual attitudes of high P scorers are a little like those of high E scorers, and also a little like those of high N scorers; the degree of similarity does not amount to more than about 8 per cent or 9 per cent of the variance. High E scorers are somewhat more markedly unlike high N scorers; the degree of dissimilarity amounts to something like 17 per cent of the variance. The within-sex comparisons are no different on the whole from the between-sex comparisons, and all are in good agreement with each other. The between-scale correlations are clearly lower than the within-scale correlations, demonstrating that our results are consistent across sex. On the whole these figures are very encouraging; they suggest that different personality types do indeed have different attitudes toward sex, regardless of the sex of the respondent.

among women (4, 20, 11, 22), perhaps unexpectedly. Masturbation is more a male pastime (10, 8), and men are also less prudish in general (18, 68, 69, 59), and feel less guilt (25). Most of these differences are not unexpected, although one should not overinterpret them; some of the replies may represent little but widely held views unthinkingly endorsed. The only unexpected feature of the study is the apparent satisfaction of the women with their sex lives; it used to be thought that the 'permissive' society favoured men, as did the Victorian era. Possibly the clue lies in the greater sex drive apparent in the men, and the difficulties which this strong drive must give rise to when confronted with the stark reality that over half the women in our sample were still virgins and apparently intent on holding on to this status. In this sellers' market, women clearly have the upper hand, and may enjoy this status; again the nature of our sample may be responsible for a finding which is not likely to be duplicated for older men and women. There is an interesting finding in Schofield's book (Ref. 11), in which he showed that female adolescents who had had intercourse were not very attractive on the whole, while male adolescents who had had intercourse were; the explanation presumably is again in terms of the sellers' market—men must be attractive to get a girl, but a girl who is attractive does not need to trade her virginity for male attention. Specific research devoted to a clarification of these relations might be of considerable interest.

RESULTS: SEXUAL PATHOLOGY

Two questions in the inventory related to sexual reactions which might be considered medically pathological, although use of this term is of course somewhat arbitrary in this context. The questions relating to male subjects were numbers 95 and 96, as shown in the Appendix; they are concerned with impotence and ejaculatio praecox respectively. For the women, these two questions referred instead to frigidity (from a = never to f = always) and orgasm during intercourse (from a = very often to f = never). The actual wording of the possible answers (a to f) was identical to that of the male questions. The wording of the female questions was: Have you ever suffered from frigidity? and Do you usually have orgasm during intercourse? These questions are only meaningful for respondents who have in fact had intercourse, and were only answered by them; in consequence they could not be included in the factor analysis, and results are discussed separately in this section.

The distributions of replies, as expected, are very asymmetrical, and in order to make possible the use of t tests an attempt was made to divide the distribution at a point which would give as nearly as possible groups of equal size; this aim was not accomplished with any very great success, due to the piling up of data in certain categories. Nevertheless, the results are suitable for statistical treatment. The male results will be discussed first, followed by the female results. In each case, the P, E and N scores of the groups which showed or did not show the pathological behaviour in question were calculated and compared, significance of differences being assessed by means of the t technique.

(1) *Male impotence*

The great majority of men gave answer (a), i.e., 'never', to this question ($n = 164$); consequently all other answers were grouped together to form the 'pathological' group ($n = 120$). Mean scores on P, E and N are shown in Table 7; it will be seen that impotent men are somewhat (non-significantly) higher on P, more introverted, and significantly ($p < 0{\cdot}05$) higher on N.

(2) *Ejaculatio Praecox*

A majority of men gave answers (e) and (f), i.e. never or hardly ever ($n = 152$); consequently all other answers were grouped together to form the 'pathological' group ($n = 132$). Mean scores on P, E and N are shown in Table 7; it will be seen that men suffering somewhat from ejaculatio praecox are slightly (non-significantly) lower on P, slightly more introverted, and significantly higher on N.

(3) *Female frigidity*

The great majority of women gave answer (b), i.e., once or twice; this was grouped with answers (c) to (f) to constitute the 'pathological' group, with those answering 'never' (a) constituting the non-pathological group. Mean scores on the personality dimensions are given in Table 7; frigid women (using this term somewhat inaccurately for our 'pathological' group) are somewhat more introverted, but not significantly so, and score higher on N, but also not significantly so. Numbers are only 49 in the non-pathological group, and 122 in the pathological group; had the numbers been as large as those in the male groups, these differences might have reached significance. Clearly repetition of the study with larger numbers is called for.

(4) *Orgasm*

Many women gave answer (a), i.e., 'very often' or (b), i.e., 'often'; these were combined to form the non-pathological group ($n = 83$).

The other answers were combined to form the 'pathological' group (n = 86). Neither P nor E seem to be related to orgasm frequency; N, however, differentiates the two groups at the 0·05 level of statistical significance. Higher N scores go with lower orgasm frequency.

The results of this analysis are not unexpected; it is found that sexual pathology as defined here is associated with neuroticism (significantly in three cases out of four, and almost significantly in the fourth case). Introverts show slightly greater pathology, but these differences never reach significance. High P scorers do not differ significantly from low P scorers, and may in fact have slightly less pathology as regards these indices of behaviour.

TABLE 7

MEAN P, E AND N SCORES OF STUDENTS PATHOLOGICAL AND NON-PATHOLOGICAL, WITH RESPECT TO FOUR SEXUAL DISORDERS

		P	*E*	*N*
1. Male Impotence:	Non-pathological	4·37	13·09	10·58
	Pathological	4·82	12·65	11·84
2. Ejaculatio	Non-pathological	4·62	13·04	10·54
Praecox:	Pathological	4·48	12·70	11·70
3. Frigidity:	Non-pathological	3·00	12·59	12·05
	Pathological	2·80	11·58	13·41
4. Orgasm:	Non-pathological	3·06	11·87	12·29
	Pathological	2·77	11·84	13·75

It is doubtful if the behaviours called 'pathological' really deserve this name, in view of the frequency with which they occur in this normal group, and it seemed of some interest to study the personality correlates of the much smaller more extreme groups giving more definitely pathological reactions. Five males admitted to having suffered from impotence often, more often than not, or always; they showed a markedly elevated P score of 7·00, which is significantly higher than average. The E score of this group fell to 11·9, and the N score rose to 12·8; these changes are in line with expectation, but not significant in view of the very small size of the sample. Six women admitted to frigidity often, more often than not, or always. Their P scores went up to 4·58, and their N score reached the very high value of 17·83; the latter value is significant beyond the 1 per cent level, but the former is not significantly different from average. The other extreme groups do not add anything of interest to the data already presented. It is interesting that in spite of the small size of the sample of frigid women, the greater degree of pathology involved has now made the relation with N significant. We may conclude, therefore, that all four types of sexual pathology are related to N, but that P is only involved significantly with high frequency of impotence.

GENERAL DISCUSSION

There would be little point in repeating the many detailed findings which this study has given rise to, or in summarizing the various conclusions. Discussion will be confined to two main points: (1) the problems of sampling and (2) the problem of veridical report. The correlations here established between sexual attitudes and personality variables are meaningful only in so far as they can be considered to transcend the particular sample on which they were established. Correlations are not as subject to sampling distortions as are population parameters such as means, but nevertheless some evidence is required to show that our sample is not so highly selected with respect to relevant variables as to make the conclusions of doubtful generality. Eysenck (Ref. 3) has shown that the sample is very similar to unselected population samples of similar age with respect to percentage of men and women with experience of coitus, and also with respect to the scores on P, E and N. In other words, our sample is representative of the population of unmarried adolescents of 18 to 22 years of age with respect to the two main variables we are concerned with, i.e., sexual experience and personality; it seems unlikely that our data are entirely idiosyncratic and unrepresentative. No doubt some distortion of sampling has taken place through the act of volunteering and other associated factors, but these are probably not so serious as to invalidate the results.

As regards veridical reports, we have two lines of argument. The first relates to internal evidence; thus, duplicated items gave very highly correlated results, which suggests that items were not filled in randomly or with intention to deceive. The large number of comments written on the questionnaire returned suggested that respondents took the task very seriously. Most important, meaningful factors are not likely to arise from an analysis of correlations between items which were not in fact completed with some degree of honesty. Furthermore, the higher correlations between sexual behaviour patterns and personality in males are unlikely to have arisen from faked data.

More convincing perhaps are various bits of external evidence. If the relations established in this paper are real, then it should be possible to find evidence in the literature of factual consequences of these relations. Eysenck (Ref. 3) has argued, for instance, that if extraverts are in fact more promiscuous, then V.D. patients and unmarried mothers should be particularly extraverted; Eysenck (Ref. 6) and Wells (Ref. 14) have found evidence in favour of these predictions. Sex differences in line with our results have been discovered in an experimental investigation by Sigurt *et al.* (Ref. 12). Psychiatrists have repeatedly found a relation between neurosis and sexual pathology; our data are very much in line with these suggestions. Ultimately, of course, there can be no absolute proof for the veridical nature of the answers given, but such evidence as has been quoted makes it unlikely that the data seriously misrepresent the truth. After all, respondents were assured of anonymity and had no motivation to tell lies; furthermore, much concentrated work was required to fill in the various questionnaires properly and post them back to the author, and few people would be likely to undertake all this just in order to mislead.

It might also be pointed out that other writers, using different methods, have reported results which, where comparable, were similar to ours. Mention has already been made of the work of Giese and Schmidt; we might also mention the interviewing studies of Schofield (Ref. 11), and of Bynner (Ref. 1), which also resulted in congruent results. There is thus beginning to build up a set of findings linking personality factors with sexual attitudes and behaviours which seems to hang together and be reproducible from study to study, even when different methods of information gathering and different samples, of different nationality, are involved. Finally, it should be noted that these results are for the most part in excellent agreement with prediction from theory; respondents could hardly have known these theories, or filled in their inventories in such a way as to support prediction!

If we can accept that the results are along the right lines, even though of course requiring replication, and relevant only to unmarried adolescents of between 18 and 22, then we can frame certain general conclusions. Sexual attitudes and behaviours seem to coalesce around two main and relatively independent factors: sexual pathology and sexual libido. Both these factors denote continua; pathology may be present to varying degree, and libidinal strength may vary from little to great. High N scorers are clearly most likely to suffer from sexual pathology; this emerges, for both men and women, from both the factor analysis and also from the separate analysis of frigidity, orgasm frequency, impotence and ejaculatio praecox. High P scorers, while also slightly prone to pathology, are particularly high on libido. Extraverts are somewhat higher on libido than introverts, and somewhat less pathological, but we have argued that this pathological association with introversion may be found only in this particular age range. As pointed out before, both the high N and the high P attitudes are probably undesirable; healthy and acceptable reactions, although entirely different, are those of extraverts and introverts, adopting respectively the hedonistic and the stoic philosophies (or the permissive and the Victorian point of view, if these terms be preferred). These are of course only the bold outlines of the picture; much of the finer detail has been disclosed in the body of this paper. If more questions are raised than answered, this should be blamed on the relative neglect of this whole field by psychologists and psychiatrists alike; it seems odd that 70 years after Freud insisted so dramatically on the importance of the study of sexual impulses so little should be known about this vital topic.

SUMMARY

Some 800 unmarried male and female students were administered a personality inventory measuring psychoticism, extraversion and neuroticism, as well as a 98-item questionnaire of sexual attitudes. Factor analysis showed that some 15 facts were sufficient to account for the attitudes sampled; most of these were similar for the two sexes. High and low scorers on the three personality variables were compared for their responses to the attitude items, and numerous highly significant differences were found; similarly, male and female students' responses were compared. Personality scores were found to be correlated with some of the sex attitude factors. In general, high N scorers showed the greatest degree of pathology, followed by high P scorers; extraverts showed an absence of pathology. P scorers showed strong libidinal desires. These and many other findings are considered in the context of the writer's personality theory which had provided certain tentative predictions about the sexual attitudes and behaviour of different personality types.

REFERENCES

1. Bynner, J. M., The association between adolescent behaviour and attitudes as revealed by a new social attitude inventory. London: Univ. of London, unpublished Ph.D. thesis, 1969.

2. EYSENCK, H. J., *The Biological Basis of Personality*. Springfield, Ill: C. C. Thomas, 1967.
3. ——, Personality and sexual behaviour. *J. psychosom. Res.*, **16,** 141–152, 1972.
4. —— & EYSENCK, S. B. G., A factorial study of psychoticism as a dimension of personality. *Multivariate Behav. Res.*, Special Issue, 15–31, 1968.
5. —— ——, *The Structure and Measurement of Personality*. London: Routledge & Kegan Paul, 1969.
6. EYSENCK, S. B. G., Personality and gain assessment in childbirth of married and unmarried mothers. *J. ment. Sci.*, 417–30, 1961.
7. EYSENCK, S. B. G. & EYSENCK, H. J., The measurement of psychoticism: a study of factor stability and reliability. *Brit. J. soc. clin. Psychol.*, **7**, 286–94, 1968.
8. —— ——, 'Psychoticism' in children: a new personality variable. *Res. in Educ.*, **1**, 21–37, 1969.
9. —— ——, Scores on three personality variables as a function of age, sex, and social class. *Brit. J. soc. clin. Psychol.*, **8**, 69–76, 1969.
10. GIESE, H. & SCHMIDT, A., *Studenten Sexualität*. Hamburg: Rowohlt, 1968.
11. SCHOFIELD, M., *The Sexual Behaviour of Young People*. London: Pelican Books, 1968.
12. SIGURT, V., SCHMIDT, G., RHEINFELD, S. & WEIDEMANN-SUTOR, I. Psycho-sexual stimulation: sex differences. *J. Sex Res.*, **6**, 10–24, 1970.
13. THORNE, F. C., The sex inventory. *J. clin. Psychol.*, Monogr. Suppl. No. 21, 1966.
14. WELLS, B. W. P., Personality characteristics of V.D. patients. *Brit. J. soc. clin. Psychol.*, **8**, 246–52, 1969.

APPENDIX

INVENTORY OF ATTITUDES TO SEX

This questionnaire is anonymous, to encourage truthful answers

Read each statement carefully, then underline the 'yes' or the 'no' answer, depending on your views. If you just cannot decide, underline the '?' reply. Please answer *every* question. There are no right or wrong answers. Don't think too long over each question; try to give an immediate answer which represents your *feelings* on each issue. Some questions are similar to others; there are good reasons for getting at the same attitude in slightly different ways.

	Percentage 'YES' Answers	
	Male:	Female:
1. The opposite sex will respect you more if you are not too familiar with them.	38	59
2. Sex without love ('impersonal sex') is highly unsatisfactory.	49	80
3. Conditions have to be just right to get me excited sexually.	21	43
4. All in all I am satisfied with my sex life.	40	60
5. Virginity is a girl's most valuable possession.	16	24
6. I think only rarely about sex.	4	13
7. Sometimes it has been a problem to control my sex feelings.	46	44
8. Masturbation is unhealthy.	7	21
9. If I loved a person I could do anything with them.	55	46
10. I get pleasant feelings from touching my sexual parts.	61	37
11. I have been deprived sexually.	25	8
12. It is disgusting to see animals having sex relations in the street.	5	6
13. I do not need to respect a woman, or love her, in order to enjoy petting and/or intercourse with her.	43	12
14. It is all right for children to see their parents naked.	64	74
15. I am rather sexually unattractive.	10	5

	Percentage 'YES' Answers Male:	Female:
16. Frankly, I prefer people of my own sex.	3	2
17. Sex contacts have never been a problem to me.	35	41
18. It is disturbing to see necking in public.	12	23
19. Sexual feelings are sometimes unpleasant to me.	11	16
20. Something is lacking in my sex life.	50	26
21. My sex behaviour has never caused me any trouble.	43	36
22. My love life has been disappointing.	39	23
23. I never had many dates.	36	26
24. I consciously try to keep sex thoughts out of my mind.	2	7
25. I have felt guilty about sex experiences.	29	41
26. It wouldn't bother me if the person I married were not a virgin.	68	73
27. I had some bad sex experiences when I was young.	15	13
28. Perverted thoughts have sometimes bothered me.	28	18
29. At times I have been afraid of myself for what I might do sexually.	19	26
30. I have had conflicts about my sex feelings towards a person of my own sex.	16	9
31. I have many friends of the opposite sex.	71	80
32. I have strong sex feelings but when I get a chance I can't seem to express myself.	23	12
33. It doesn't take much to get me excited sexually.	66	31
34. My parents' influence has inhibited me sexually.	30	25
35. Thoughts about sex disturb me more than they should.	12	7
36. People of my own sex frequently attract me.	4	4
37. There are some things I wouldn't want to do with anyone.	53	47
38. Children should be taught about sex.	94	97
39. I could get sexually excited at any time of the day or night.	88	69

	Percentage 'YES' Answers Male:	Female:
40. I understand homosexuals.	44	35
41. I think about sex almost every day.	84	52
42. One should not experiment with sex before marriage.	7	21
43. I get sexually excited very easily.	60	27
44. The thought of a sex orgy is disgusting to me.	18	65
45. It is better not to have sex relations until you are married.	6	31
46. I find the thought of a coloured sex partner particularly exciting.	24	3
47. I like to look at sexy pictures.	61	8
48. My conscience bothers me too much.	18	26
49. My religious beliefs are against sex.	7	13
50. Sometimes sexual feelings overpower me.	32	27
51. I feel nervous with the opposite sex.	25	15
52. Sex thoughts drive me almost crazy.	6	2
53. When I get excited I can think of nothing else but satisfaction.	24	15
54. I feel at ease with people of the opposite sex.	66	80
55. I don't like to be kissed.	2	3
56. It is hard to talk with people of the opposite sex.	12	6
57. I didn't learn the facts of life until I was quite old.	26	23
58. I feel more comfortable when I am with my own sex.	24	16
59. I enjoy petting.	92	78
60. I worry a lot about sex.	22	13
61. The Pill should be universally available.	84	65
62. Seeing a person nude doesn't interest me.	11	43
63. Sometimes thinking about sex makes me very nervous.	16	20
64. Women who get raped are often partly responsible themselves.	57	53
65. Perverted thoughts have sometimes bothered me.	26	18
66. I am embarrassed to talk about sex.	9	8

	Percentage 'YES' Answers Male:	Female:
67. Young people should learn about sex through their own experience.	34	23
68. Sometimes the woman should be sexually aggressive.	88	64
69. Sex jokes disgust me.	4	22
70. I believe in taking my pleasures where I find them.	44	7
71. A person should learn about sex gradually by experimenting with it.	52	42
72. Young people should be allowed out at night without being too closely checked.	68	54
73. Did you ever feel like humiliating your sex partner?	20	12
74. I would particularly protect my children from contacts with sex.	5	9
75. Self-relief is not dangerous so long as it is done in a healthy way.	74	56
76. I get very excited when touching a woman's breasts.	57	45
77. I have been involved with more than one sex affair at the same time.	32	14
78. Homosexuality is normal for some people.	74	70
79. It is all right to seduce a person who is old enough to know what he or she is doing.	73	35
80. Do you ever feel hostile to your sex partner?	37	40
81. I like to look at pictures of nudes.	63	10
82. Buttocks excite me.	42	8
83. If you had the chance to see people making love, without being seen, would you take it?	41	12
84. Pornographic writings should be freely allowed to be published.	59	32
85. Prostitution should be legally permitted.	62	32
86. Decisions about abortion should be the concern of no one but the woman concerned.	52	47
87. There are too many immoral plays on TV.	6	13
88. The dual standard of morality is natural, and should be continued.	32	26

	Percentage 'YES' Answers Male:	Female:
89. We should do away with marriage entirely.	9	2
90. Men marry to have intercourse; women have intercourse for the sake of marriage.	7	3
91. There should be no censorship, on sexual grounds, of plays and films.	63	39

Please underline the correct answer

92. If you were invited to see a 'blue' film, would you: (a) Accept (b) Refuse	80	37
93. If you were offered a highly pornographic book, would you: (a) Accept it (b) Reject it	76	40
94. If you were invited to take part in an orgy, would you: (a) Take part (b) Refuse	61	4

95. Given availability of a partner, would you prefer to have intercourse:
(a) Never
(b) Once a month
(c) Once a week
(d) Twice a week
(e) 3–5 times a week
(f) Every day
(g) More than once a day

96. Have you ever suffered from impotence?
(a) Never
(b) Once or twice
(c) Several times
(d) Often
(e) More often than not
(f) Always

97. Have you ever suffered from ejaculatio praecox (premature ejaculation)?
(a) Very often
(b) Often
(c) Middling
(d) Not very often
(e) Hardly ever
(f) Never

98. At what age did you have your first intercourse?

10

Crime and Personality: Item Analysis of Questionnaire Responses[1]

SYBIL B. G. EYSENCK & H. J. EYSENCK

First published in
British Journal of Criminology, **11**, 49–62, 1971

INTRODUCTION

IN a preceding article Eysenck & Eysenck (Ref. 3) have outlined the three-factor theory linking personality and criminal behaviour, and have published evidence in support of the hypothesis that criminals, in comparison with non-criminals, are characterized by high scores on the psychoticism (P), extraversion (E) and neuroticism (N) scales of a new questionnaire constructed, validated and standardized by the writers (Refs. 6 & 7). It was argued in this paper that scale scores may not always reveal all the important information contained in a set of comparisons, and that an analysis of all the individual items, comparing experimental and control groups, might throw some additional light on the problems concerned. The present article presents such a comparison, using the same information employed in our preceding paper, but analysing items instead of scales.

Obvious though the suggestion of using items in comparing criminals and normals may be, only one study has come to hand which has in fact employed this technique. The study in question was conducted by Sanocki (Ref. 9), who used the short form of the MPI (Ref. 1) on eighty-four Polish prisoners and 337 Polish controls, matched for age, education and social class. Criminals were found to be significantly more extraverted ($p < 0{\cdot}01$), and non-significantly more neurotic. Only 14 per cent of controls were 1 SD above the mean for E, but 44 per cent of criminals. Out of the twelve questions in the inventory, significant differences were observed in five; three of these are measures of E, two of N. Criminals said 'Yes' more frequently to the following questions:

[1] We are indebted to the Home Office for permission to test prisoners; most of the testing was carried out by prison psychologists to whom we wish to express our gratitude for their generous help. Opinions expressed are of course our own, and do not represent the view of the Home Office.

Do you like plenty of excitement and bustle around you? Are you rather lively? Can you usually let yourself go and enjoy yourself at a gay party? Would you call yourself tense or 'highly strung'? Controls said 'Yes' more frequently to the following question: Do you suffer from sleeplessness? (This last difference is in a direction contrary to hypothesis.) It is interesting to note that the item: Do you like mixing with people? did not differentiate significantly between the groups; this is in agreement with the hypothesis put forward in the preceding article to the effect that it is the impulsivity aspect of extraversion, rather than the sociability aspect, which differentiates criminals from controls.

Sanocki's results are not dissimilar to those reported in our previous paper, except that they are more clear-cut and significant with respect to E, and less so with respect to N. In part this may be due to the fact that different types of prisoners in his study were found to differ significantly with respect to their inventory scores; thus differences in the composition of the two groups of criminals could account for these incongruities.[1] Sanocki also found that prisoners' behaviour in prison correlated significantly with E; extraverts offended significantly more frequently against prison rules. He does not report item analyses for these additional findings.

THE INVESTIGATION

A specially constructed personality inventory (the PI) was administered to 603 male prisoners with a mean age of 22·1 years; it was also administered to three control groups. Group A consisted of 532 male non-prisoners, all married and contacted through a random sampling of groups of schoolchildren who were asked to obtain the co-operation of their parents for a project unconnected with the present investigation; this is a fairly representative group of the general population, except for age (mean age 44·6 years) and for the obvious exclusion of unmarried and childless males. Group B consisted of 423 university students with a mean age similar to that of the criminals, but of course somewhat

[1] Because of the small numbers involved, Sanocki only gives figures for three groups of criminals, viz. those imprisoned for theft ($n = 19$), robbery ($n = 31$) and murder ($n = 6$). Most extraverted was the first group (77 per cent above the mean); the second group was significantly ($p < 0{\cdot}01$) less extraverted (36 per cent above the mean). The murderers were the most introverted group of all, with four out of six having introverted scores. The numbers are of course small, and the results require replication before they can be accepted as being in any sense representative; nevertheless they are of some interest in opening up this particular area of investigation.

higher social class membership, and higher intelligence. Group C consisted of 185 industrial apprentices, aged 17·9 years on average; all students and apprentices were male. None of these groups is ideal as a control group; it was hoped that the possibility of multiple comparisons would make up for the defects of any single group. In interpreting the results, it should therefore be remembered that Group A is older and more settled; hence its members are likely to be somewhat more introverted, and less high on N and P, than would be a random sample of young males. Students are known to be rather high on N, and possibly somewhat lower on E, than a random sample. Apprentices, being the youngest group, are known to be exceptionally high on E, and possibly somewhat lower on N than a random group.

The inventory used consists of eighty questions; it is reproduced in the appendix in order to make possible a meaningful discussion of individual questions. Several factor analyses were done on the intercorrelations between these items, using a variety of different populations from whom results were available; these guided us in selecting items to make up the P, E and N scales. Three items had reasonably high loadings on more than one scale, and were accordingly scored for two scales. The key used is given with the inventory in the appendix, so as to make replication of this research possible.

RESULTS

The best way of discussing results is perhaps by taking in turn the items measuring the three main factors with which the inventory is concerned. We shall start with P. (Table 1 sets out the percentage 'Yes' replies of the four groups.) It is clear that for most of these items there is a marked difference in the predicted direction between criminals and all three control groups; this applies to questions 3, 9, 15, 21, 24, 34, 37, 41, 43, 47, 51 and 68; these hardly call for an extended discussion. More interesting perhaps is a consideration of why the remaining items fail to differentiate. Four items (5, 13, 26, 39) are rather similar; they deal with hurting people and animals. Possibly prisoners give conventional answers to these questions; it is known from unpublished work with a Lie scale that prisoners tend to have high Lie scale scores, and these four questions perhaps resemble Lie scale score items in some respects. This may also be true of item 19 (Did you love your mother?); prisoners may be reluctant to admit something so obviously frowned upon by society. Item 32 (Would you take drugs?) is similar to item 19 in that it calls for a response which is clearly unconventional, to say the least, and singles the respondent out as abnormal. Item 45 has loadings both on P (negative) and on N (positive); these two tendencies may cancel out in prisoners who are supposed to be high on both P and N. Items 55, 62, 71, 74 and 79 also do not differentiate, and here again there is some reason to suggest that they may resemble Lie scale items in that they ask for conventional modes of reply. It should of course be emphasized that the hypotheses outlined above must be regarded as nothing more than *ad hoc* suggestions for future investigation; thus the inclusion of a Lie scale would make possible the testing of our hypothesis that some of the P items are not endorsed by prisoners in the appropriate direction because of their similarity to L items.

TABLE 1

ITEMS ON THE P SCALE: PERCENTAGE OF KEYED ANSWERS FOR CONTROL AND PRISONER GROUPS

Item	Controls			
	A	B	C	D
3	11·24	7·33	5·41	13·31
5	4·68	9·93	4·86	5·49
9	13·86	15·13	10·27	47·25
13	14·98	27·66	30·27	19·13
15	8·05	11·35	16·76	27·29
−19	93·63	88·89	96·76	88·35
21	11·99	9·69	9·73	26·62
24	23·97	19·15	26·49	67·22
−26	98·50	90·31	89·73	94·18
32	1·12	26·00	7·03	16·64
−34	93·26	90·31	96·22	78·70
37	22·66	13·00	16·22	58·24
−39	94·57	87·47	89·19	90·35
41	3·56	1·89	1·62	9·48
43	5·43	8·51	9·19	21·96
−45	51·87	71·63	58·38	57·07
−47	97·19	95·98	99·46	90·68
51	11·05	13·00	22·16	43·26
−55	95·69	73·76	91·35	93·51
62	29·59	33·33	30·81	25·79
−68	77·72	77·07	68·65	57·07
−71	88·76	73·76	83·24	83·36
−74	38·58	46·34	48·11	48·75
79	21·16	37·59	54·59	26·12

Scores on N seem to fall into two fairly clear-cut categories—some items differentiate very well between criminals and controls, others if anything show the criminals inferior with respect to N. A consideration of the items in question may throw some light on this problem. Items differentiating well are the following: 22 (Worry about things should not have said or done); 35 (Troubled about feelings of guilt); 38 (Tense or highly strung); 50 (Palpitations or thumping of heart); 61 (Worries about awful things that might happen); 70 (Nervous person); 78 (Worries about health). To these might be added, although with rather less confidence, the following items: 10 (Moods go up and down); 14 (Feels just miserable for no good reason); 25 (Feelings rather easily hurt); and 46 (Ideas run through head). The non-differentiating items are: 1 (Long for excitement)—this is also an E item; 2 (Needs understanding friends to cheer up); 18 (Suddenly feel shy); 28 (Sometimes energetic, sometimes sluggish); 31 (Daydreams); 42 (Thinks he could have done better); 58 (Irritable); 60 (Different thoughts come into mind); 73 (Easily hurt); and 76 (Feelings of inferiority). It is possible to suggest the hypothesis that items which differentiate criminals from controls are of an autonomic type, i.e., referring to direct manifestations of sympathetic arousal, or else to introspective interpretations of such arousal in the form of worry, or feelings of tenseness, being 'highly strung', nervous, etc. The non-differentiating items do not seem to carry this interpretation. Here again it must of course be recognized that we are merely dealing with a *post hoc* interpretation of observed differences, and that the hypothesis suggested above requires to be established in properly planned researches before any credence can be given to it. Table 2 shows the figures on which the above argument is based.

We now turn to the E items, details concerning which are given in Table 3.[1] An effort has been made here to test the hypothesis, mentioned

[1] It is interesting to note here that Gibson (Ref. 8) has published some figures which suggest that criminals (unlike controls) tend to *under-state* their extraversion when 'faking good' (as indicated by high scores on the Lie scale). No Lie scale was used in the present study, but unpublished work has shown that prisoners in fact have high scores on such a scale, suggesting that possibly they are 'faking good' to a greater extent than would be true of the various control groups used. If this were true, then it might be suggested that the 'true' P and N scores of the prisoners would be even higher than those reported here; and if Gibson's interesting finding could be replicated, then it might also be found that E scores were similarly underestimates of the 'true' values. We do not wish to press this point, as even without any corrections for 'faking' the responses of criminals are clearly differentiated from those of the controls; nevertheless it seems likely that our findings are minimum estimates of the true differences in personality between prisoners and controls.

in the previous paper, that items relating to sociability would discriminate less well than items relating to impulsiveness, using as our guide to this distinction the results of previous factor analyses (Ref. 5). Of the items which could reasonably be regarded as relating to sociability, the majority either do not discriminate (27, 75), or if anything discriminate

TABLE 2

ITEMS ON N SCALE: PERCENTAGE OF KEYED ANSWERS FOR CONTROL AND PRISONER GROUPS

Item	Controls			
	A	B	C	D
1	42·70	71·87	74·59	70·88
2	24·16	53·43	49·73	51·75
10	47·00	63·83	63·78	65·22
14	40·26	65·72	48·11	53·08
18	38·20	63·83	52·97	48·75
22	50·56	61·94	62·16	74·71
25	51·12	55·32	37·30	54·91
28	54·31	73·29	71·89	60·73
31	27·72	63·59	42·70	30·62
35	28·28	26·95	44·32	64·23
38	25·66	22·46	7·03	31·95
42	63·11	78·25	72·43	66·06
45	51·87	71·63	58·38	57·07
46	43·07	56·97	43·24	55·41
50	20·41	37·35	36·22	44·59
58	27·72	29·08	16·76	23·79
60	52·81	71·16	58·92	57·07
61	22·28	25·77	23·78	47·42
70	17·23	26·95	10·81	31·28
73	55·81	50·83	41·08	48·25
76	21·91	37·12	24·86	26·96
78	17·60	13·95	22·16	37·10

in the wrong direction (23, 30, 36, 44, 48). Items 66, 69 and 77 show the criminals as more sociable. It is possible that the first two of these may not be uninfluenced by the peculiar restrictions on talking and social intermingling which characterize the life of the prisoner; both refer to seeing and talking with people. Item 77 might be considered as referring to impulsiveness rather than to sociability, depending on whether one pays more attention to the activity involved (getting life into a dull party), or rather the attendance at the party itself. However we may decide on these points, the fact remains that *in toto* the items here collected together as referring to sociability fail to discriminate on the whole between criminals and controls. The position is quite different when we turn to the items concerned with impulsiveness. Positive

TABLE 3

ITEMS ON THE E SCALE: PERCENTAGE OF KEYED ANSWERS FOR CONTROL AND PRISONER GROUPS

Item	Controls			
	A	B	C	D
1	42·70	71·87	74·59	70·88
4	59·18	52·72	64·86	67·39
−8	88·01	71·16	80·54	65·56
12	26·22	38·06	34·05	56·57
16	14·23	16·78	15·14	21·13
20	47·38	64·78	64·32	72·71
−23	34·83	13·00	8·11	21·96
27	42·70	84·63	90·81	85·02
−30	65·92	59·57	55·14	68·22
33	61·61	61·70	70·27	51·41
36	61·05	78·25	88·11	80·70
40	49·06	50·59	62·16	69·05
−44	51·12	31·68	34·05	63·56
−48	45·88	30·50	25·41	35·44
−56	60·86	38·77	32·97	44·26
59	61·61	71·16	78·38	65·06
66	16·10	10·87	14·59	23·63
69	27·15	48·46	54·05	61·23
72	86·33	68·79	79·46	76·87
−75	33·15	21·75	7·03	19·63
77	34·27	37·59	53·51	64·89
79	21·16	37·59	54·59	26·12

discrimination is given by the great majority (items 4, 8, 12, 16, 20, 40), with only three items going in the wrong direction (33, 59 and 72). Items 33 and 72 might have been influenced by prison experiences; shouting back when someone shouts at you is not encouraged in prison, and self-confidence is unlikely to flourish under prison conditions. Again, these suggestions may or may not be acceptable; clearly they are *post hoc*, and difficult to prove. On the whole, however, the impulsiveness items clearly do differentiate between criminals and controls in a manner not found in the case of the sociability items.[1]

A small number of items was included in the inventory, but not scored for any of the scales, either because their loadings on the factor in question were not high enough, or because the items had loadings on more than one factor, such that including it would have interfered with the orthogonality of the factors. However, for the purposes of an item analysis these considerations do not seem relevant, and consequently these items are analysed in Table 4. Some of them clearly do not differentiate (items 7, 49, 52, 57 and 65); the majority, however, do differentiate reasonably well. Items 6, 11, 17, 29, 53, 54, 63, 64, 67 and 80 suggest that criminals, as compared with controls, don't find it hard to take no for an answer, worry about catching illnesses, let their dreams warn or guide them, think that people take offence easily, get attacks of shaking or trembling, think that people try to avoid them, wonder if people really mean it when they are friendly to them, have many nightmares, are troubled by aches and pains, and suffer from sleeplessness. Most of these items had loadings on the P and/or N scales; it is interesting to note that the sleeplessness item, which in the Sanocki study mentioned in the introduction scored in the wrong direction, here scores in the right direction. These items, in so far as interpretation is concerned, support our original hypothesis that criminals would have higher P and N scores.

It is clear that while on the whole the detailed analysis presented above supports our three-factor theory, individual items are subject to many other influences external to those which make them part of a particular factor, and that consequently factor or scale scores give much less clear discrimination than could be obtained from combinations of items made on the basis of item analysis. It seemed interesting

[1] It is interesting to note that this finding agrees with a re-analysis carried out on some of our data relating extraversion to eye-blink conditioning (Ref. 4). It will be remembered that Eysenck's (Ref. 2) original theory postulated that extraverts tended to be over-represented among criminal groups because of defects in their nervous system which made them less easy to condition, and thus form the socialized habits which make up what we usually call 'conscience'. The finding that criminals are distinguished from controls with respect to the impulsivity, rather than the sociability aspect of extraversion suggests a similar relationship with conditioning, and re-analysis of our data has indeed shown that the correlation between eye-blink conditioning and extraversion is mediated by the impulsivity items in the scale, rather than by the sociability ones. The complementary nature of these findings suggests that our original suggestion may have been along the right lines, but not sufficiently specific with respect to the precise aspect of personality involved.

to try to see to what extent our criminal groups could be differentiated from our normal control groups when the most discriminating items from our inventory were combined into a scale irrespective of their factor loadings, and purely based on the results of the item analysis. Such a scale would of course capitalize on random sampling errors, and to that extent exaggerate the discriminating power it possesses; however, with numbers of subjects as large as those in our various groups

TABLE 4

ITEMS NOT ON P, E OR N SCALES: PERCENTAGE OF KEYED ANSWERS FOR CONTROL AND PRISONER GROUPS

Item	A	B	C	D	
6	48·88	51·06	49·19	34·94	N*
7	89·70	94·33	97·84	89·52	E
11	7·87	8·75	8·65	20·47	P
17	6·37	9·69	8·65	18·47	P
29	19·66	18·20	18·38	33·28	P
49	35·39	54·14	36·76	35·61	N
−52	84·46	66·90	89·19	81·70	E
53	13·48	21·04	16·76	29·45	P
54	8·05	16·08	8·11	21·80	N
57	59·18	61·70	60·00	62·73	P
63	33·15	41·37	46·49	57·74	P
64	3·18	4·73	3·78	14·31	N
65	27·34	27·42	18·92	24·46	E
67	19·85	12·77	8·11	19·97	N
80	12·92	22·46	15·68	34·78	N

* Letters indicate scales items would belong to according to highest factor loadings

this danger is not a very real one. In any case, the scale presented is intended mainly for future experimental use; the figures to be given regarding it, when applied to the sample from which it was derived, are only to be regarded as suggestive. Only replication with other groups is likely to teach us the limitations to which the scale is subject.

The scale has 40 items: these are marked with a 'C' in the appendix. Scores on this scale were calculated for all four groups; these, together with their SDs, are given below in Table 5. KR 20 reliabilities were also established for each of the groups; these too are given in Table 5. On this 'criminal propensity' scale the control groups have reasonably similar scores, with the middle-aged fathers as expected having the lowest scores; criminals have very much higher scores, the difference exceeding one SD. These results suggest that this scale might with advantage be tried on pre-criminal populations (i.e., to assess its predictive value), and that it might be used on an experimental basis for prediction of parole success. Correlations with 'troublesomeness' within prison might also be of interest. However, the main interest of the results given in Table 5 rests on the clear demonstration of personality differences between prisoners and controls, even when both groups are taken in this completely undifferentiated manner.

TABLE 5

	Mean	SD	Reliability
Control group A	9·46	4·80	0·77
Control group B	10·39	4·36	0·70
Control group C	10·67	4·28	0·70
Prisoners	16·65	5·73	0·78

The reliabilities quoted do not suggest the existence of any marked differences between criminal and normal groups with respect to the homogeneity of this hypothetical 'criminal propensity' allegedly measured by the scale; such differences as appear are clearly a function of the higher variance of prisoners' scores, which in turn is a function of their higher mean scores. The failure of the test reliabilities of the prisoners to be clearly superior to those of the control groups suggests interesting theoretical interpretations. If it is true, as we have suggested, that prisoners differ from controls with respect to three orthogonal personality dimensions (P, E and N), then two alternative hypotheses suggest themselves.

(1) According to the three-factor hypothesis, some criminals would differ from the controls on P, others on E, and others yet on N; occasionally some prisoners might differ on two or even three scales, but this would not occur more frequently than chance combination of independent scores would allow. On this hypothesis, the three factors would be as independent among criminals as among controls.

(2) According to an alternative hypothesis, one might suggest the possibility that in order to become a criminal it is necessary to possess not just one of these three personality characteristics in excess, but have all three to above-mean degree. On this hypothesis criminals would constitute a very special highly-selected population taken

largely from one octant of the three-dimensional space generated by our three personality factors. In such a group the orthogonality of the three factors would be lost, and it might be predicted that the reliability as a combined score, such as our 'criminal propensity' score, would be increased. The fact that this has not happened suggests that this 'combined factor' hypothesis does not give an entirely accurate account of the situation, and that P, E and N are partly independent and additive, rather than combinatorial and multiplicative, factors in predisposition to criminal activity.

SUMMARY AND CONCLUSIONS

This paper has provided evidence that the differentiation between personality features of criminals and controls is possible, even when both groups are left completely undifferentiated with respect to such factors as specific crimes committed. The evidence further suggests that existing scales of personality types, such as P, E and N, may be too broad to give maximum differentiation between groups, and that detailed item analyses may succeed in separating out component lower-order factors within these higher-order concepts which produce greater differentiation between groups. Such differentiation may also be helpful theoretically, and suggests further experimental and analytical work; the suggestion that the impulsivity rather than the sociability aspects of extraversion are involved with criminality, and the consequent discovery that a similar distinction obtains with respect to eye-blink conditioning, may be quoted as one example of such mutual interdependence.

Observed differences, although quite substantial in some cases, are probably minimum estimates of the 'true' personality differences which exist between prisoners and controls. Prisoners are characterized by elevated scores on 'Lie scales' constructed for the purpose of detecting 'faking good' tendencies among testees, and in view of the known correlations between these scores and P and N scores any reasonable correction applied to the observed figures would increase them by something like 15 to 20 per cent at least. The same might be true of the E scores; these are usually uncorrelated with L scores in normal populations, but the situation seems to be different for criminals (Ref. 8). Thus for all three scales used in this inquiry, reported results are likely to give an underestimate of the 'true' personality differences existing between our experimental and control populations.

Interesting though these findings are, they probably also underestimate the degree of discrimination possible because in these studies we have treated all prisoners as a homogeneous group, irrespective of type of crime, severity of crime, length of sentence, recidivism, or any other feature which distinguishes one criminal from another. Sanocki has demonstrated that prisoners are heterogeneous with respect to personality, and that much improved discrimination could be obtained by bearing this fact in mind, and analysing data with respect to more homogeneous groupings of prisoners. This clearly must be the next development.

REFERENCES

1. Eysenck, H. J., A short questionnaire for the measurement of two dimensions of personality. *J. Appl. Psychol.*, **42**, 14–17, 1958.
2. ——, Symposium: The development of moral values in children. VII. The contribution of learning theory. *Brit. J. Educ. Psychol.*, **30,** 11–21, 1960.
3. —— & Eysenck, S. B. G., Crime and personality: an empirical study of the three-factor theory. *Brit. J. Criminol.*, **10,** 225–239, 1970.
4. —— & Levey, A. (1967). 'Konditionierung, Introversion-Extraversion und die Stärke des Nervensystems.' *Zeit. für Psychol.*, **174,** 96–106.
5. Eysenck, S. B. G. & Eysenck, H. J., On the dual nature of extraversion. *Brit. J. Soc. Clin. Psychol.*, **2,** 46–55, 1963.
6. ————, The measurement of psychoticism: A study of factor stability and reliability. *Brit. J. Soc. Clin. Psychol.*, **7,** 286–294, 1968.
7. ————, Scores on three personality variables as a function of age, sex and social class. *Brit. J. Soc. Clin. Psychol.*, **8,** 69–76, 1969.
8. Gibson, H. B., The significance of 'lie responses' in the prediction of early delinquency. *Brit. J. Educ. Psychol.*, **39,** 284–290, 1969.
9. Sanocki, W., The use of Eysenck's inventory for testing young prisoners. *Przeglad penitencjarny*, (*Warszawa*), **7,** 53–68, 1969.

PERSONALITY INVENTORY

Name.................................... Age.............. Sex.................

Occupation ....

INSTRUCTIONS

Please answer each question by putting brackets around the 'YES' or the 'NO' following the question. There are no right or wrong answers, and no trick questions. Work quickly and do not think too long about the exact meaning of the question.

REMEMBER TO ANSWER EACH QUESTION

1.		Do you often long for excitement?	YES	NO
2.		Do you often need understanding friends to cheer you up?	YES	NO
3.	C	Do most things taste the same to you?	[YES]	NO
4.	C	Are you usually carefree?	[YES]	NO
5.		Do you enjoy hurting people you love?	YES	NO
6.	C	Do you find it very hard to take no for an answer?	[YES]	NO
7.	C	Do you generally feel well?	YES	[NO]
8.	C	Do you stop and think things over before doing anything?	YES	[NO]
9.	C	Have you had more trouble than most?	[YES]	NO
10.		Does your mood often go up and down?	YES	NO
11.	C	Do you worry a lot about catching illnesses?	[YES]	NO
12.	C	Do you generally do and say things quickly without stopping to think?	[YES]	NO
13.		Do you sometimes like teasing animals?	YES	NO
14.		Do you ever feel 'just miserable' for no good reason?	YES	NO
15.	C	Are there people who wish to harm you?	[YES]	NO
16.	C	Would you do almost anything for a dare?	[YES]	NO
17.	C	Do you let your dreams warn or guide you?	[YES]	NO
18.		Do you suddenly feel shy when you want to talk to an attractive stranger?	YES	NO
19.		Did you love your mother?	YES	NO

20. C	Do you often do things on the spur of the moment?	[YES]	NO
21. C	Is there someone else who is to blame for most of your problems?	[YES]	NO
22. C	Do you often worry about things you should not have done or said?	[YES]	NO
23.	Generally do you prefer reading to meeting people?	YES	NO
24. C	Would you have done better if people had not put difficulties in your way?	[YES]	NO
25.	Are your feelings rather easily hurt?	YES	NO
26.	Would it upset you a lot to see a child or animal suffer?	YES	NO
27.	Do you like going out a lot?	YES	NO
28.	Are you sometimes bubbling over with energy and sometimes very sluggish?	YES	NO
29. C	Do people generally seem to take offence easily?	[YES]	NO
30.	Do you prefer to have few but special friends?	YES	NO
31.	Do you daydream a lot?	YES	NO
32.	Would you take drugs which may have strange or dangerous effects?	YES	NO
33.	When people shout at you, do you shout back?	YES	NO
34. C	Was your father a good person?	YES	[NO]
35. C	Are you often troubled by feelings of guilt?	[YES]	NO
36.	Can you usually let yourself go and enjoy yourself a lot at a gay party?	YES	NO
37. C	Are you usually very unlucky?	[YES]	NO
38. C	Would you call yourself tense or 'highly-strung'?	[YES]	NO
39.	Would you feel very sorry for an animal caught in a trap?	YES	NO
40. C	Do other people think of you as being very lively?	[YES]	NO
41. C	When you are in a crowd, do you worry about catching germs?	[YES]	NO
42.	After you have done something important, do you often come away feeling you could have done better?	YES	NO

43. C	Do your friendships break up easily without it being your fault?	[YES]	NO
44. C	Are you mostly quiet when you are with other people?	YES	[NO]
45.	Do you care a lot about what others think of you?	YES	NO
46.	Do ideas run through your head so that you cannot sleep?	YES	NO
47. C	Was your mother a good person?	YES	[NO]
48.	If there is something you want to know about, would you rather look it up in a book than talk to someone about it?	YES	NO
49.	Do you very often just sit and do nothing?	YES	NO
50. C	Do you get palpitations or thumping in your heart?	[YES]	NO
51. C	Do people tell you a lot of lies?	[YES]	NO
52.	Do you like the kind of work that you need to pay close attention to?	YES	NO
53. C	Do you think some people try to avoid you?	[YES]	NO
54. C	Do you get attacks of shaking or trembling?	[YES]	NO
55.	Do good manners and personal cleanliness matter much to you?	YES	NO
56.	Do you hate being with a crowd who play jokes on one another?	YES	NO
57.	When things go wrong is it usually your own fault?	YES	NO
58.	Are you an irritable person?	YES	NO
59.	Do you like doing things in which you have to act quickly?	YES	NO
60.	Do a lot of different thoughts often come into your mind when you are trying to talk to someone?	YES	NO
61. C	Do you worry about awful things that might happen?	[YES]	NO
62.	Are you slow and unhurried in the way you move?	YES	NO
63. C	When people are friendly do you wonder whether they really mean it?	[YES]	NO
64. C	Do you have many nightmares?	[YES]	NO
65.	Do you normally speak rather loudly?	YES	NO

66. C Do you like talking to people so much that you never miss a chance of talking to a stranger?	[YES]	NO
67. C Are you troubled by aches and pains?	[YES]	NO
68. C Do you generally understand why people feel the way they do?	YES	[NO]
69. C Would you be very unhappy if you could not see lots of people most of the time?	[YES]	NO
70. C Would you call yourself a nervous person?	[YES]	NO
71. Do you try to be rude to people?	YES	NO
72. Would you say that you were fairly self-confident?	YES	NO
73. Are you easily hurt when people find fault with you or your work?	YES	NO
74. Before taking decisions, do you generally ask someone's advice?	YES	NO
75. Do you find it hard to really enjoy yourself at a lively party?	YES	NO
76. Are you troubled with feelings of inferiority?	YES	NO
77. C Can you easily get some life into a rather dull party?	[YES]	NO
78. C Do you worry about your health?	[YES]	NO
79. Do you like playing pranks on others?	YES	NO
80. C Do you suffer from sleeplessness?	[YES]	NO

Please check to see that you have answered all the questions.

Part Three:
The Experimental Study of Extraversion

11

Cortical Inhibition, Figural Aftereffect and Theory of Personality

H. J. EYSENCK[1]

First published in
Journal of Abnormal and Social Psychology, **51**, 94–106, 1955

THE formulation of a complete theory of personality must be based on the discovery of invariances of two rather different types. In the first place, what is required is *static* or *descriptive* invariance, i.e., the taxonomic, nosological, or dimensional analysis of personality. Work of this kind would result in a descriptive system of personality in terms of a limited number of abilities, traits and attitudes; in the exact sciences the most obvious analogue to this system would be the discovery of the Periodic Table of Elements. The statistical methods involved in studies of this kind would be those making use of analysis of interdependence (correlational analysis, component analysis, association and contingency analysis, factor analysis).

In the second place, what is required is *dynamic*, or *sequential* invariance, i.e., the analysis of lawful sequences of behaviour and the discovery of their causes. Work of this kind would result in a causal system of laws in terms of concepts such as conditioning, inhibition, oscillation, etc.; in the exact sciences the most obvious analogue to this would be the discovery of the laws of motion. The statistical methods involved in studies of this kind would be those making use of analysis of dependence (analysis of variance and covariance, regression analysis and confluence analysis).

As has been pointed out elsewhere (Ref. 5), a logical case can be made out for maintaining that the *static* type of analysis should precede the *dynamic*; before we can discover dynamic laws responsible for extra-

[1] The writer is indebted to the Bethlem Royal Hospital and the Maudsley Hospital Research Committee for a grant which made this study possible. Dr L. Minski, Superintendent of Belmont Hospital, and Dr M. Desai, Chief Psychologist, gave permission for patients to be tested and very kindly helped in the selection of patients, as did various psychiatrists at Belmont Hospital, to all of whom thanks are due. Numerous discussions with Mr M. B. Shapiro clarified many theoretical problems and the writer is indebted to Mr A. E. Maxwell for statistical help and advice.

version, say, or neuroticism, we must demonstrate that these concepts do in fact refer to measurable and operationally definable entities. Work summarized in *The Structure of Human Personality* has shown that many different investigators holding divergent points of view and making use of a great variety of test procedures can be found to agree with respect to their main conclusions in the taxonomic field. The following six points present a brief summary of the main areas of agreement:

1. Human conduct is not specific, but presents a certain amount of *generality*; in other words, conduct in one situation is predictable from conduct in other situations.

2. Different degrees of generality can be discerned, giving rise to different levels of personality organization of structure. It follows that our view of personality structure must be *hierarchical.*

3. Degrees of generality can be operationally defined in terms of correlations. The lowest level of generality is defined by test-retest correlations; the next level (trait level) by intercorrelations of tests purporting to be measures of the same trait, or the same primary ability; the highest level by correlations between different traits defining second-order concepts like g in the cognitive field and 'neuroticism' in the orectic field, or type concepts like extraversion-introversion.

4. Mental abnormality (mental deficiency, neurosis, psychosis) is not qualitatively different from normality, in the sense that a person with a broken arm, or a patient suffering from haemophilia, is different from someone not ill; different types of mental abnormality constitute the extreme ends of continuous variables which are probably orthogonal to each other.

5. It follows from the above that psychiatric diagnostic procedures are at fault in diagnosing categories, such as 'hysteria' or 'schizophrenia'; what is required is the determination of the main dimensions involved and a quantitative estimate of the patient's position on each of these dimensions (see example below).

6. The main dimensions involved in the analysis of personality for which sufficient experimental data are available to make possible a theoretical formulation are neuroticism and extraversion-introversion.

While the congruence of empirical findings in this field is welcome, it should not be allowed to disguise from us the fact that the task of personality theory cannot stop halfway. We would be well advised to regard traits, types, abilities, attitudes and 'factors' generally not as the end products of our investigation, but rather as the starting point for a more causal type of analysis. Thurstone has pointed out that a coefficient of correlation is a confession of ignorance (Ref. 44); it indicates the existence of a relation but leaves the causal problem quite indeterminate. Much the same is true of a statistical factor; based, as it is, on an analysis of a set of correlations, it still does not in itself reveal to us anything about the causal relations at work. In this paper, therefore, an attempt is made to go beyond the purely descriptive studies which have so far engaged the main attention of our laboratory and to attempt the construction of a causal hypothesis with respect to at least one of the main personality dimensions.

Extraversion and the Cortical Inhibition Hypothesis

A brief summary of an experimental investigation will indicate the type of fact calling for an explanation. Proceeding on the hypothesis that the test differences between hospitalized neurotics and nonhospitalized 'normals' (i.e., people without psychiatric involvement) would provide us with an outside criterion of 'neuroticism' and that test differences between hysterics (Jung's prototype group for the concept of 'extraversion') and dysthymics (patients suffering from anxiety, Jung's prototype group for the concept of 'introversion') would provide us with an outside criterion of 'extraversion-introversion', a battery of objective tests of persistence, suggestibility and other traits was administered to groups of hysterics, psychopaths, reactive depressives, obsessionals, anxiety states, mixed neurotics and normals (Ref. 13). Retaining the hysterics, anxiety states and normals as criterion groups, intercorrelations were calculated between tests for the subjects in the remaining groups, and a Lawley-type factor analysis was performed. Three clear-cut simple structure factors emerged, corresponding to intelligence, neuroticism and extraversion. Intelligence tests had high loadings on the intelligence factor; the tests differentiating between the normal and neurotic groups had high loadings on the neuroticism factor; the tests differentiating between the hysterics and anxiety states had high loadings on the extraversion-introversion factor.

Factor scores on the introversion-extraversion factor were then calculated for the persons in the various groups. Fig. 20 gives a diagrammatic indication of the results obtained. The line separating the neurotic groups from the normal subjects was drawn so as to put 10 per cent of the normal group on the neurotic side, this being the percentage found by R. Fraser to show debilitating neurotic tendencies in a normal working-class population (Ref. 8). It will be seen that psychopaths are slightly more extraverted than hysterics and that obsessionals and

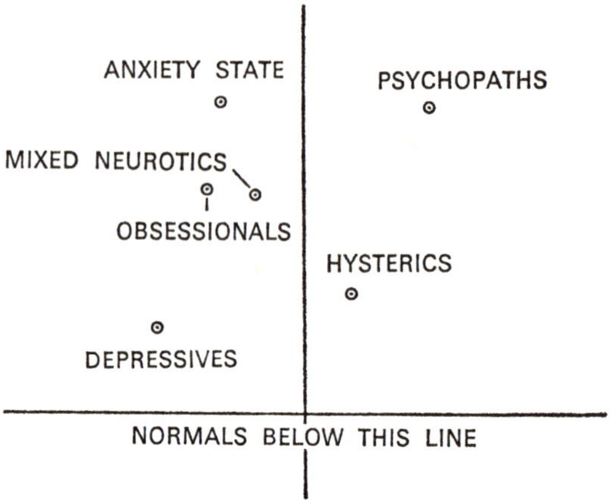

Figure 20. Empirically determined positions of group means for neurotic patients diagnosed as reactive depression, obsessional, anxiety state, mixed, hysteric, and psychopath, respectively.

depressives are about as introverted as anxiety states. Differences between extraverted groups and introverted groups are fully significant. Mixed neurotics are intermediate between the other groups; normals are very significantly lower on 'neuroticism' than any of the neurotic groups. These results allow us to use the hysteric-psychopath group on the one hand and the dysthymic group (anxiety state, reactive depression, obsessionals) on the other as criteria for any predictions made in terms of a theory of extraversion-introversion.

One further fact is relevant in connection with any hypothesis regarding extraversion-introversion. In a study of monozygotic and dyzygotic twins, McLeod has shown that a factor of extraversion-introversion (in addition to other factors) could be obtained from the intercorrelation of a large number of objective tests (Ref. 24); he also found that the intercorrelation of factor scores was very much higher for the monozygotic than for the dyzygotic twins. This indicates that extraversion is strongly based on an inherited disposition. If we are willing to use Holzinger's coefficient h^2 as a very rough index of the contribution of heredity to the variance of our extraversion measure in this sample, we would have to conclude that the contribution of heredity is very much stronger than that of environment.

This finding suggests that our search for a causal factor responsible for extraverted behaviour should be concentrated on properties of the central nervous system and more particularly the cortex, as it is unlikely that peripheral factors could be responsible for the far-reaching and complex differences observed between extraverts and introverts. Historically there have been several attempts in this direction; we need only mention the work of Gross on the primary and secondary function (Refs. 10 & 11) and that of Spearman on perseveration (Ref. 41). Experimental evidence is not lacking to show that these early attempts were quite unsuccessful; the recent work of Rim, for instance, has shown not only that there is no one general factor of perseveration but also that none of the 20 or so tests of perseveration used by him succeeded in differentiating at a reasonable level of significance between hysterics and dysthymics (Ref. 34).

More acceptable, perhaps, is a theory proposed by Pavlov, who considered the phenomena of hysteria to be closely linked with his concept of *inhibition.* Postulating excessive concentration of excitation in a weak nervous system, Pavlov argues that in the hysteric the process of negative induction should give rise to intense inhibition effects (Ref. 26). His theory is difficult to follow in detail and testable deductions cannot easily be made with any confidence. Further, Pavlov did not extend his tentative hypothesis to the typological field, nor did he himself carry out any experimental work on human beings to support or refute it. Nevertheless, the theory here presented is essentially a development and simplification of his. It bases itself on the concept of *reactive inhibition* developed by Hull (Ref. 17), rather than on that of *negative induction* developed by Pavlov (Ref. 27), because the evidence in favour of the former appears more conclusive than the evidence in favour of the latter and also because the former seems to lend itself more easily to the formulation of exact and testable predictions.

We may state this theory in three parts, dealing respectively with the general law, the postulation of individual differences and the typological postulate. The general law reads as follows:

A. *Whenever any stimulus-response connection is made in an organism (excitation), there also occurs simultaneously a reaction in the nervous structures mediating this connection which opposes its recurrence (inhibition).* This hypothesis is a more general formulation of Hull's first submolar principle; it states in effect, as he puts it, that

> 'all responses leave behind in the physical structures involved in the evocation, a state or substance which acts directly to inhibit the evocation of the activity in question. The hypothetical inhibitory condition

or substance is observable only through its effect upon positive reaction potentials. This negative action is called *reaction inhibition.* An increment of reactive inhibition (ΔI_R) is assumed to be generated by every repetition of the response (R), whether reinforced or not and these increments are assumed to accumulate except as they spontaneously disintegrate with the passage of time.'

The second part of the hypothesis deals with the problem of individual differences adumbrated by Pavlov but almost completely neglected by Hull. A statement of this part of the hypothesis might be as follows:

B. *Human beings differ with respect to the speed with which reactive inhibition is produced, the strength of reactive inhibition and the speed with which reactive inhibition is dissipated. These differences themselves are properties of the physical structures involved in the evocation of responses.*

The third part of the hypothesis relates A and B to the results of taxonomic work summarized above and states:

C. *Individuals in whom reactive inhibition is generated quickly, in whom strong reactive inhibitions are generated and in whom reactive inhibition is dissipated slowly are thereby predisposed to develop extraverted patterns of behaviour and to develop hysterical disorders in cases of neurotic breakdown; conversely, individuals in whom reactive inhibition is generated slowly, in whom weak reactive inhibitions are generated and in whom reactive inhibition is dissipated quickly, are thereby predisposed to develop introverted patterns of behaviour and to develop dysthymic disorders in cases of neurotic breakdown.*

Comparatively little work has been done in this field since Pavlov's original fragmentary hypotheses were formulated. The experiments by Welsh & Kubis (Refs. 45 & 46) have lent some support to hypotheses of this type. In one experiment these investigators used PGR conditioning on 82 control subjects and 51 neurotic patients. They found, as could be predicted from the inhibition theory, that their patients, most of whom were of the dysthymic type, conditioned very much more quickly than did the controls (average number of repetitions required for the production of a conditioned response was $8{\cdot}6 \pm 3{\cdot}1$ in the patients and $23{\cdot}9 \pm 8{\cdot}2$ in the controls). Among the patients an attempt was made to rate the degree of anxiety from which they were suffering; it was found that the average number of repetitions required to produce a conditioned response in those with great and moderate anxiety was 7·1 and 8·4 respectively; in those with mild or no anxiety the number of repetitions required was 22·2 and 26·3. (Correlations between conditionability and age and intelligence were quite insignificant; test-retest reliability was 0·88 in the normal group.)

In another experiment 24 dysthymic patients were contrasted with 22 controls. Again the mean number of repetitions required was significantly different for the two groups, being $7{\cdot}5 \pm 2{\cdot}31$ for the dysthymic patients and $21{\cdot}86 \pm 7{\cdot}97$ for the controls. Some hysterics were also tested and were found difficult to condition.

The only investigation, however, to put the hypothesis to a proper test by including a matched group of hysterics as well as normal and dysthymic groups was carried out at the Maudsley Hospital by Franks (Ref. 7). Using the eyewink reflex to a puff of air as the response and a tone as the conditioned stimulus, he obtained unequivocal evidence that dysthymics condition more quickly than normals and normals more quickly than hysterics. (The normal group, being a random sample of the population, would include extraverts and introverts in roughly equal proportions and would therefore be ambivert on the average and consequently intermediate between the extravert-hysteric and the introvert-dysthymic groups.)

Among several other investigators who have succeeded in relating speed of conditioning to dysthymia, the work of Taylor (Ref. 42) and Taylor & Spence (Ref. 43) is of particular interest, as these investigators advance an explanation of the phenomenon which is somewhat different from our own.

Making use of Hull's formula ${}_{s}E_{r} = {}_{s}H_{r} \times D$, where ${}_{s}E_{r}$ represents excitatory potential, ${}_{s}H_{r}$ represents habit strength and D represents drive strength, they argue that anxiety is related to drive level and that consequently higher states of anxiety should lead to quicker conditioning (${}_{s}E_{r}$) because of increases in drive strength (D). Their experiments do not provide crucial evidence with respect to the two theories involved as the same prediction would be made in terms of both hypotheses.[1] It

[1] Taylor and Spence (Ref. 43) use the Taylor Scale of Manifest Anxiety as a measure of anxiety in spite of the fact that little evidence is brought forward to support any assumption that it correlates with clinical estimates of anxiety. The work of Holtzman (Ref. 2), as well as that of Sampson & Bindra (Ref. 35), in which an attempt is made to link up scores on this scale and independent criteria, fails to support Taylor's hypothesis. Franks has shown that contrary to the Taylor and Spence hypothesis hysterics, whose scores on the Taylor scale are about as high as those of dysthymics, are more difficult to condition than members of a normal group, whose scores on the Taylor Scale are very much lower (Ref. 7). He also failed, as have other investigators (Refs. 2 & 14), to obtain a significant correlation between conditioning and score on the Taylor Scale. These findings throw considerable doubt on the Taylor-Spence hypothesis.

seemed necessary, therefore, to choose a prediction which would produce positive effects in terms of our hypothesis, but where no such prediction could reasonably be made in terms of the Taylor-Spence hypothesis. An attempt to formulate such a deduction will be made in the next section.

CORTICAL INHIBITION AND FIGURAL AFTEREFFECT

In searching for a phenomenon which would avoid the ambiguity of results encountered in the work of conditioning, it was found necessary to go back from Hull's development of learning theory to Pavlov's somewhat more fundamental position. Pavlov regarded the conditioned reflex as a tool for investigating the dynamics of cortical action rather than as a paradigm of learning. He considered that the laws discovered by him had perfectly general validity and were not restricted to the very special circumstances of the conditioning experiment; indeed, he suggested explicitly that perceptual and other phenomena could find an explanation in terms of inhibition, excitation, disinhibition, etc. It seems possible, therefore, that we may be successful in our search if we look for perceptual phenomena to which our general theory may be found applicable.

The phenomenon chosen for this purpose was the figural aftereffect discussed by Köhler & Wallach (Ref. 20), Gibson (Ref. 9), Luchins (Ref. 23) and others in a series of articles. Essentially, the effects observed showed beyond doubt that constant stimulation of parts of certain sensory surfaces, such as the retina, sets up states of inhibition in corresponding areas in the cortex which have measurable effects on the perception of stimuli later presented in the same region. If, for instance, a circle is fixated for a period of one or two minutes and is then withdrawn, other stimulus objects, such as a small square, appearing within that part of the retina and the cortex which had previously been surrounded by the circle, will appear smaller than a square of precisely the same size appearing elsewhere on the retina and the cortex.

Effects of this kind appear to be exactly in line with the statement quoted in explanation of Part A of our hypothesis to the effect that 'all responses leave behind in the physical structures involved in the evocation, a state or substance which acts directly to inhibit the evocation of the activity in question' (Ref. 17). It should be noted that in accepting the fact of the occurrence of figural aftereffects, we need not necessarily accept Köhler's theory regarding the origin of these aftereffects, just as in accepting the fact of Pavlovian inhibition we need not accept his theory of cortical inhibition. There is, indeed, a curious resemblance between the arch-atomist Pavlov, on the one hand and the arch-Gestaltist Köhler, on the other, in that both have proposed what are strictly physiological, molecular theories of brain action to account for their findings and that both theories are well outside orthodox neurology. Konorski has discussed the relationship between Pavlov's physiological and neurological theories and those of Sherrington and other orthodox workers in some detail and has attempted to account for Pavlov's experimental results in more acceptable terms (Ref. 21); Osgood and Heyer (Ref. 25) have attempted to do a similar service for Köhler's figural aftereffects.

While we need not deal in detail with Köhler's theories, we must note the terminology used by him, which is in part at least bound up with his theory. The reader will find a more extensive discussion in a recent paper by Luchins & Luchins (Ref. 23). Briefly, then, Köhler assumes that every visual figure is associated with currents in the visual sector of the nervous system, the currents being the results of a difference in density and brightness between figure and ground. (For ease of discussion we are presenting an example from the visual field, but the same arguments apply to all other sensory fields, and the experiment to be described shortly was, indeed, done in the kinaesthetic field rather than in the visual.) The visual sector is considered as a volume conductor and figure currents are assumed to polarize all surfaces through which they pass. This polarization and certain aftereffects in the affected cells are called *electrotonus* and it is known that this condition of electrotonus may proceed for some time after the polarizing current has ceased to flow. Köhler uses the term *satiation* to describe electrotonic effect of figure currents on the cortical sector; the term *figural aftereffects* is used to denote the alterations which test objects may show when their figure currents pass through a satiated region.

Satiation has as its main effect a localized inhibition in the sense that polarization of the affected cells increases their resistance to the passage of an electric current, thereby making the appearance of figure currents in that region more difficult, i.e., acting as an inhibiting agent. The main observable fact mediated in this way is the *displacement* of test objects from the affected region. This displacement is measurable, shows pronounced individual differences and may be used both as a measure and as an operational definition of cortical inhibition in the perceptual field.

The importance of these satiation phenomena in their own right will be obvious to anyone familiar with Köhler's highly original and brilliant work in this field. From the point of view of general psychology, they are of particular interest in that they form a bridge between two large fields of study which have hitherto remained either out of touch or else frankly antagonistic to each other. One of these is the field of conditioning and learning theory; the other is that of perception. In this work on figural aftereffects we find at long last a *rapprochement* between these large groups of workers and the sets of facts unearthed quite independently by them and it is encouraging to note that the general law of inhibition enunciated by Pavlov and more explicitly by Hull, appears to be formally identical with that advanced by Köhler in terms of perceptual satiation.[1] As long as we regard only the speculative brain theories of these writers, we will tend to miss the essential similarity of their formulations; once we concentrate on the molar rather than on the molecular parts of their theories the similarity will be striking.

The main aim of this section, however, is not to point to similarities between Pavlovian and Gestalt theories, but rather to link both of these with personality theory. From what has been said above it follows immediately that if our argument is sound and if the 'reactive inhibition' of Pavlov and Hull is indeed essentially identical with the factors involved in Köhler's 'satiation', then it would follow directly from Parts B and C of our theory that hysterics should show satiation effects more markedly than dysthymics. In fact, three quite specific predictions can be made. In the first place, satiation effects should appear *earlier* in the hysteric group; in the second place, they should appear more *strongly* in the hysteric group; and in the third place, they should disappear more *slowly* in the hysteric group. These are quite specific predictions which can be tested experimentally and it is only through such experimental verification that the theory can show its acceptability and usefulness. Our next section will, therefore, be concerned with certain empirical results obtained in comparing a group of hysterics and a group of dysthymics with respect to figural aftereffects.

AN EXPERIMENTAL TEST OF THE CORTICAL INHIBITION HYPOTHESIS: METHOD

Apparatus

The apparatus used in this experiment is an adaptation of that described by Köhler & Dinnerstein (Ref. 19); the exact form of apparatus

[1] Several workers in Great Britain have recently shown interest in attempts to bring together into one framework these two great fields (Refs. 1 & 3).

and procedure was taken from Klein & Krech (Ref. 18), who used it in their work on cortical conductivity in the brain-injured. As a full description and rationale are given by these authors, our own will be brief.

The apparatus consists of a comparison scale, a test object and a stimulus object. Movable riders are affixed to all three objects in such a way that the position of thumb and forefinger is fixed as the subject moves these two fingers up and down along the sides of the object. All objects are made of unpainted, smoothed hardwood. The apparatus is so arranged as to present the comparison scale to the left of the seated subject and either the test or stimulus object to his right.

Procedure

The subject (S) is blindfolded before he has an opportunity of viewing any part of the equipment. Having taken his seat in front of the apparatus, his task is explained in detail and a demonstration given. Then the experiment proper commences. Putting thumb and forefinger of his right hand into the rider on the test object and thumb and forefinger of his left hand into the rider on the comparison scale, S is required to adjust the position of the rider on the comparison scale until the distance between the fingers of his left hand feels equal to the distance between the fingers of his right hand. This is the point of subjective equality and all changes are measured from this point as the baseline. Four separate determinations are carried out and the results averaged, to make this baseline more reliable.

The next step in the experiment consists in providing S with varying periods of constant tactile stimulation. For this purpose he is instructed to put his fingers into the rider on the stimulus object, which is slightly broader than the test object ($2\frac{1}{2}$ in. as compared with $1\frac{1}{2}$ in.) and to rub the sides of the stimulus object at an even rate for periods of 30 sec, 60 sec and 120 sec, respectively. Four determinations of subjective equality are made after each period of rubbing, in order to obtain more reliable measures. In this way the effect of rubbing the stimulus object on the perception of the test object is ascertained. Finally, after 5 minutes rest and again after another 10 minutes rest, the subjective width of the test object is again ascertained in order to establish the perseverative effects of the stimulation periods. These two sets of judgments are again obtained four times each in order to increase reliability.

Scoring

The predicted aftereffect consequent upon the rubbing of a stimulus object *broader* than the test object is an apparent shrinking of the test object, which should manifest itself in terms of a decrement in the width on the comparison scale judged equal to the test object. For each subject this decrement is expressed in terms of his own original baseline, so that individual differences in perceived equality are taken into account in the score, which thus is essentially a percentage decrement score, i.e., an estimate of the shrinkage that has occurred as a percentage of the original width of the object as perceived by each subject.

The following scores will be reported in this paper: (1) average percentage decrement after 30 sec; (2) average percentage decrement after 60 sec; (3) average percentage decrement after 90 sec; (4) average percentage decrement after 120 sec; (5) sum of the above four scores; (6) maximum single percentage decrement obtained from any subject. In addition to these poststimulation aftereffects, the following recovery period scores were obtained: (a) average percentage decrement after a 5 minute rest; (b) average percentage decrement after (10 minutes+5 minutes =) 15 minutes rest; (c) sum of these two scores.

Subjects

The Ss used in this investigation were selected on the basis of two criteria. The first of these was that they should fall into the diagnostic groups of hysterics and dysthymics respectively. Diagnoses of conversion hysteria, hysteria and psychopathy were accepted as falling into the former group; diagnoses of anxiety state, reactive depression, obsessional and compulsive disorders were accepted as falling into the latter group.

In view of the known unreliability of psychiatric diagnosis, which has been demonstrated, for instance, in *The Scientific Study of Personality* (Ref. 4), it was considered advisable to have a second criterion which was independent of diagnosis. For this purpose a questionnaire was used which had been shown by Hildebrand to be a good measure of extraversion (Ref. 13). This questionnaire is Guilford's Rhathymia scale (Ref. 12) and the reader will find evidence regarding the adequacy of this scale as a measure of extraversion discussed elsewhere (Ref. 6). The procedure followed was that no one with a score below 31 was accepted as extraverted and no one with a score above 39 was accepted as introverted.[1] While it would have been desirable to have no overlap at all in

[1] Hysterics were found by Hildebrand to have an average score of 37 ± 12, dysthymics one of 28 ± 10 (Ref. 13). In our sample the means were 40 ± 12 and 25 ± 10 respectively.

the questionnaire scores of the two groups, it proved impossible to find a large enough group of subjects in the time available to reach this ideal. We can only suggest that the results found with the present groups would probably have been improved somewhat if a stricter criterion could have been employed.

TABLE 1

POSTSTIMULATION FIGURAL AFTEREFFECTS—DYSTHYMICS

Source	df	MS	F
Between times	3	116·0082	0·7752
Between people	13	2050·0241	13·7010
Residual	39	149·6416	
Total	55		
$r_{11} = 0{\cdot}9270$			

TABLE 2

RECOVERY PERIOD AFTEREFFECTS—DYSTHYMICS

Source	df	MS	F
Between times	1	1·9137	0·0541
Between people	13	642·1574	18·1429
Residual	13	35·3945	
Total	27		
$r_{11} = 0{\cdot}9449$			

There were fourteen subjects in each group, all of them males. The average ages of the two groups were 29·14 (hysterics) and 34·23 (dysthymics), an insignificant difference. Matrix IQ's were 100·86 and 104·92, Mill Hill Vocabulary IQ's 102·79 and 110·25; these differences also were insignificant.

Reliability of Scores

Granted that our methods of scoring, which we have taken over from Klein & Krech (Ref. 18), are the most obvious ones, we must first of all ask ourselves questions regarding their reliability and consistency. To our knowledge, there are no reports in the literature dealing with this question, which is of crucial importance whenever test results are to be used as psychometric scores. Consequently, two analyses of variance were carried out for each of the two groups with whom we are concerned, i.e., the hysterics and the dysthymics. The first analysis deals with the scores which we have called average poststimulation figural aftereffects; the second analysis deals with the scores from the two recovery periods. With the formula suggested by Hoyt (Ref. 16), reliabilities of 0·93 and 0·94 were found for the dysthymics; both of these were significant at the 0·001 level. For the hysterics the reliabilities are somewhat lower, being 0·78 and 0·86 respectively. Both of these however are significant at the 0·01 level. Full details are given in Tables 1, 2, 3 and 4.[1]

TABLE 3

POSTSTIMULATION FIGURAL AFTEREFFECT—HYSTERICS

Source	df	MS	F
Between times	3	38·5519	0·3895
Between people	13	443·9761	4·4860
Residual	39	98·9703	
Total	55		
$r_{11} = 0{\cdot}7771$			

TABLE 4

RECOVERY PERIOD AFTEREFFECTS—HYSTERICS

Source	df	MS	F
Between times	1	53·8013	1·1749
Between people	13	319·8050	6·9837
Residual	13	45·7933	
Total	27		
$r_{11} = 0{\cdot}8568$			

[1] This consistency in itself poses certain problems for the theoretical analysis of the figural aftereffect phenomenon. Some subjects consistently over-rate rather than under-rate the size of the test object after stimulation. This is very difficult to account for in terms of either the Gestalt or the statistical type of hypothesis. A survey of the literature on other types of inhibition phenomena (massed and spaced learning, reminiscence, etc.) indicates that while most people act in conformity with prediction, some consistently go counter to prediction, i.e., learn better with massed rather than with spaced practice, etc. Theorists usually deal with averages rather than with individual cases and traditionally disregard aberrations of this kind. It seems reasonable to ask that any adequate theory should be able to account for discordant cases as well as for the admittedly large number of concordant ones.

Having found dysthymics to be more consistent in their test performances than hysterics, we would expect to find the correlations among the six scores (four poststimulation scores and two recovery period scores) to be higher for the dysthymics than for the hysterics; this is indeed so. On comparison of the two sets of 15 correlations pair by pair, it was found that in 13 cases the dysthymic correlation was higher; in one case the two were equal; in one case the hysteric correlation was higher. Thus, our expectation is borne out that dysthymics would be more consistent than hysterics.

RESULTS

TABLE 5

	Poststimulation Figural Aftereffects						Recovery Period		
	30 sec	60 sec	90 sec	120 sec	ϵ	Max.	5 min	10 min	ϵ
				Hysterics					
Means	9·68	10·58	13·09	12·78	46·13	20·74	4·35	8·00	12·35
Variances	9·48	13·57	14·22	16·30	1775·90	97·58	14·65	12·94	645·70
				Dysthymics					
Means	1·70	6·21	2·98	7·96	18·85	15·32	0·89	0·36	1·52
Variances	12·97	21·95	32·83	27·77	8200·10	190·12	15·77	20·59	1284·31

We must next turn to the main differences between the groups. Means and variances for hysterics and dysthymics respectively are given in Table 5 for the four poststimulation aftereffects, the sum of the poststimulation aftereffects, the maximum poststimulation aftereffects, the five and ten minute recovery period aftereffects and the sum of the rest period aftereffects. Four poststimulation aftereffects and the two rest periods are plotted in Fig. 21. All the results will be seen to be in line with prediction. Figural aftereffects in the hysteric group appear more quickly, are more strongly marked and disappear more slowly than in the dysthymics.

The significance of the differences between the two groups was tested by means of Hotelling's T test (Ref. 15). This over-all test invalidated the null hypothesis at between the 0·01 and 0·05 levels of significance. Individual one-tail t tests applied to the 9 separate scores disclosed that only the 30 sec period gave results significant at below the 0·05 level of significance; the other scores were significant at approximately the 0·10 level only. It is suggested that in future work more attention be paid to short periods of stimulation (between 10 sec and 30 sec) as longer periods

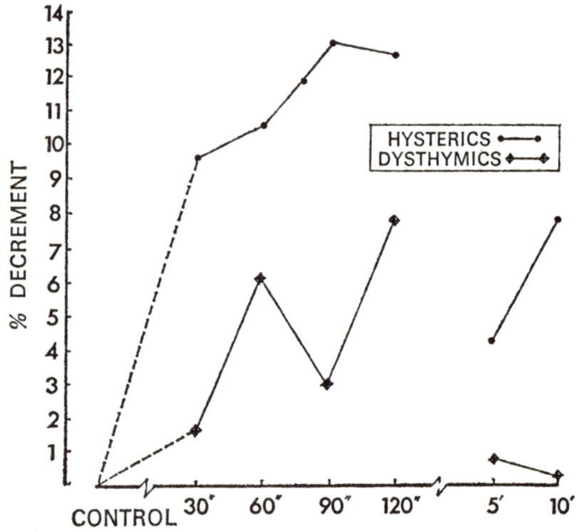

Figure 21. Amount of figural after-effect shown as percentage decrement after four different periods of stimulation and two different periods of rest.

of stimulation appear to increase variability without increasing differentiation. It might also prove useful to make use of more prolonged rest pauses; times of 15 minutes, 20 minutes and 30 minutes might give improved differentiation.

The calculation of differences between groups gives little idea of the strength of the relationship discovered. Accordingly product-moment correlations were calculated beween scores on the figural aftereffect test and the R scale. In addition to the 28 hysterics and dysthymics used for the group comparison, an additional seven neurotics were included in this calculation. These Ss had shown a discrepancy between diagnosis and score on the R scale and had therefore not been included in the group comparisons. Correlations for this group of altogether 35 neurotic subjects were as follows: 0·374 (30 sec); 0·252 (60 sec); 0·236 (90 sec);

0·218 (120 sec); 0·321 (5 minutes); 0·237 (10 minutes). It will be noted that with increasing periods of stimulation, correlations tend to fall off in a regular progression. As regards significance, the correlation for the 30 sec period almost reaches the 0·01 level; of the others only the correlation for the 5 minute rest period passes the 0·05 level of significance. The remaining correlations just fall short of the 0·05 level. Significance levels were of course calculated by using one-tailed tests, as follows from the logic of the experimental design.

It is interesting to note the fate of the seven individuals in whom diagnosis and R score disagreed. In each case where a patient was diagnosed hysteric but had an R score which put him on the introverted side, relatively small aftereffects were found. In each case where a patient was diagnosed dysthymic but had an R score which put him on the extraverted side, relatively large aftereffects were found. In other words, when diagnosis and questionnaire disagree, agreement of the experimental test is much closer with the questionnaire than with diagnosis. In view of the widespread habit of heaping contumely upon questionnaires, this fact may deserve stressing.

DISCUSSION

It will not require much discussion to establish the relevance of the results of our experiment to a theory of neurotic disorder. Psychoanalytic theories have usually played down differences between the various types of neurotic symptomatology as accidental, unimportant and variable; usually the implication has been that hysteria and the dysthymic disorders both lie close to each other along one single dimension of *regression* and that hysterical symptoms are in a sense merely a defence against the overt anxiety shown by the dysthymic. On the basis of this type of theory, no fundamental differences would be expected on psychophysiological measures of conditioning or of figural aftereffects. The fact that such differences are observed considerably weakens the Freudian theory and supports the dimensional theory outlined at the beginning of this paper. Another advantage of the dimensional theory appears to be that it can account for the similarities observed in the behaviour and the symptomatology of hysterics, brain-injured and leucotomized patients, a task not even attempted by psychoanalytic writers. A discussion of such an extension of our theory may be in order.

The experimental procedure adopted in Section 4 was taken over directly from Klein & Krech and a comparison of our results with theirs may be of some interest. They were concerned with differences between brain-injured patients and normals and found that figural aftereffect was much more strongly marked among the former than in the normal control group. The average size of the overall figural aftereffect was 12·08 per cent for the brain-injured and 6·25 per cent for the controls. The maximum degree of effect for the brain-injured averaged 19·50 per cent, for the controls, 13·00 per cent. Corresponding figures for hysterics and dysthymics are: 11·53 per cent and 4·71 per cent for average overall effect, 20·74 per cent and 15·32 per cent for maximum effect. There is thus a distinct similarity in the behaviour of the brain-injured in Klein & Krech's study and the hysterics in our own. The normal controls tested by Klein & Krech give results intermediate between our hysteric and dysthymic groups, though somewhat closer to the dysthymics.

These figures would seem to indicate similarities between hysteria and brain injury which are important from a theoretical point of view. In a series of studies (Refs. 28, 29, 30 & 31). Petrie has shown that one of the psychological aftereffects of leucotomy is an increase in extraversion, as measured by objective tests of personality similar to those used by Hildebrand in his factorial study (Ref. 13). The theory on which the prediction of a change toward extraversion after leucotomy was based was essentially one of increased cortical inhibition following brain injury.[1] Such an hypothesis is much too broad and general to account for all the known facts and will presumably require a good deal of detailed modification, particularly with respect to the differential activity of various parts of the brain and the effect of specific incisions and ablations. Thus, recent unpublished work by Petrie has shown that a change in the direction of increased extraversion is produced by all prefrontal operations involving the convexity (standard leucotomy, Rostral leucotomy and selective surgery of areas 9 and/or 10). On the other hand, cingulectomy and orbital undercutting, i.e., operations not involving the convexity, do not have aftereffects involving a shift toward extraversion on the tests used. If these results were to be confirmed, they would clearly indicate the need to make this general hypothesis much more specific.

Nevertheless, as a first approximation, this general hypothesis has

[1] Here again Pavlov's theory of negative induction has also been used to account for some of the observed effects (Refs. 36, 37, 38, 39 & 40); it is not clear to what extent negative induction and reactive inhibition can be identified with each other at the phenomenal level.

led to the prediction of the phenomena observed by Petrie (Ref. 28) and it does account similarly for the results of the Klein & Krech experiment. It would appear worthy of further investigation, particularly as it gives rise to very clear-cut predictions. Thus, we may predict that the formation of conditioned reflexes would be more difficult in the brain-injured than in the intact individual. Some evidence supporting this prediction has been published by Reese, Doss & Gantt (Ref. 33). After leucotomy, we would predict that inhibitory effects would be more strongly marked than before and we would also be able to make a number of predictions regarding the reactions of leucotomized patients on certain perceptual tests similar to those made in the concluding section of this paper with respect to hysterics.

Klein & Krech, in their paper, advance a somewhat different theory which, however, in most essentials appears to deviate but little from that used in our own work. They assume that

> . . . 'transmission rate of excitation patterns varies from individual to individual, from time to time within the same individual and from area to area within a single cortical field at any time. With this assumption it is possible to appeal to *differential* cortical conductivity as a parameter which will help us understand inter- and intra-individual differences in cortical integration and therefore in behaviour' (Ref. 18, p. 118).

It may be worthwhile to indicate in just one sentence the essential difference between the conductivity hypothesis and the one advocated here. Klein & Krech postulate neural conductivity as a basic personality dimension, assuming that it may be high or low *prior to any stimulation.* We assume that individuals differ not with respect to conductivity, but with respect to the rate at which inhibition is aroused along cortical pathways by the passage of a neural impulse. The latter hypothesis seems to be more securely based on experimental findings, less subject to unprovable assumptions and more easily testable. It is for these reasons that it has been preferred in this paper. It should be added, however, that both the conductivity and the inhibition hypotheses give rise to similar predictions in the case of the degree of satiation to be expected in the brain-injured and hysterical patients and that the data reported here do not in any way disprove the conductivity hypothesis, any more than they prove the inhibition hypothesis.

It may be worthwhile, however, to indicate very briefly the type of prediction which our theory makes possible and to suggest lines along which it could be disproved.

1. If we accept Köhler's demonstration that the rate of disappearance with time of the Müller-Lyer and other illusions is a consequence of figural aftereffects, it can be predicted that the rate of disappearance of the illusion should be more rapid with hysterics than with dysthymics and in the brain-injured as compared with the normal.

2. If we accept Klein's interpretation of the phenomenon, it can be predicted that when the persistence of an afterimage is measured as a function of the duration of stimulus exposure, the duration of the afterimage in hysterics should fall off significantly as compared with dysthymics. Klein has already shown that this is so when the brain-injured are compared with normal subjects (Ref. 18).

3. Phenomena of apparent motion may be reformulated in terms of the inhibition theory and it may be predicted that the optimal time interval for the perception of apparent movement would be decreased more in hysterics than in dysthymics after the introduction of some form of continuous stimulation in the path of the apparent movement. Shapiro has shown, in experiments using continuous stimulation in order to produce experimental inhibition effects in the occurrence of apparent movement, that under conditions of inhibition the time-interval threshold was 140 sigma, as compared with 250 sigma under noninhibition conditions (Ref. 40).

4. If a theory of satiation or inhibition be acceptable as accounting for reversal of perspective, then one would predict not only that the rate of reversal would increase in time as it is known to do but also that this increase in rate of reversal should be more marked among hysterics than among dysthymics. Our prediction here, as in the case of the experiment described in this paper, would relate more to a change of rate than to the initial rate of reversal, although the latter also should show differences in favour of the hysterics and the brain-injured.

5. Perceptual disinhibition phenomena of the type studied by Rawdon-Smith (Ref. 32) and others might be presumed also to show differences between hysterics and dysthymics. On the hypothesis that we are dealing with the inhibition of an inhibition in these cases, it might be predicted that disinhibition should be more pronounced among hysterics than among dysthymics.

6. Critical flicker fusion would be expected to be observed at different frequencies in hysterics and brain-injured, as compared with dysthymics and non-brain-injured. This follows directly from our interpretation of

the law of reactive inhibition. Some empirical data are available to support one of these predictions at least (Ref. 22).

7. Rotation phenomena, such as have been described by Shapiro (Ref. 40), have been explained by him in terms of inhibition (negative induction). If this hypothesis which has led to important discoveries in the field of brain injury, should prove acceptable, then we would expect a greater degree of rotation among hysterics than among dysthymics.

In making these predictions, we have purposely kept within the perceptual field, but it is clear that many other predictions could be made in the fields of learning, memory and motor behaviour. Phenomena of reminiscence, of massed and spaced learning, of vigilance, of blocking and many others have been interpreted in terms of inhibition. While it remains possible, of course, that in each separate case we must have recourse to a different type of inhibition, this does not seem a likely contingency and the hypothesis certainly appears worth testing that it is the same type of cortical inhibition which causes all these phenomena, as well as the perceptual ones discussed above. The obvious method of testing this hypothesis appears to be in terms of individual differences, i.e., in postulating that a person found to show a high degree of inhibition with respect to any one of these phenomena should also show a high degree of inhibition with respect to all the others. It is hoped to provide evidence with respect to this generalized inhibition hypothesis in the near future.

SUMMARY AND CONCLUSIONS

An attempt has been made in this paper to work out a dynamic theory to account for a number of experimental findings in the field of personality related to the concept of extraversion-introversion. Following Pavlov and Hull, a theory of cortical inhibition was developed to account for observed differences in behaviour and a deduction from this principle was made by extending it to the perceptual field. It was predicted that hysterics (as a prototype of the extraverted personality type) would be differentiated from dysthymics (as a prototype of the introverted personality type) in the *speed of arousal, strength and length of persistence* of figural aftereffects. A comparison of two groups of carefully selected subjects showed that (a) hysterics developed satiation and figural aftereffects more quickly than did dysthymics, (b) that hysterics developed stronger satiation and figural aftereffects than did dysthymics and (c) that hysterics developed more persistent satiation and figural aftereffects than did dysthymics. The differences are statistically significant and are in complete accord with prediction. In the discussion, certain parallels were drawn between hysteria and brain injury in terms of the theory outlined, with particular reference to the aftereffects of leucotomy. Lastly, a number of predictions were made from the theory which should permit of an experimental decision as to its validity.

REFERENCES

1. BERLYNE, D. E., Attention, perception and behaviour theory. *Psychol. Rev.*, **58,** 137–146, 1951.
2. BITTERMAN, M. E. & HOLTZMAN, W. H., Conditioning and extinction of the galvanic skin response as a function of anxiety. *J. abnorm. soc. Psychol.*, **47,** 615–623, 1952.
3. BROADBENT, D. E., Classical conditioning and human watch-keeping. *Psychol. Rev.*, **60,** 331–339, 1953.
4. EYSENCK, H. J., *The Scientific Study of Personality.* London: Routledge & Kegan Paul, 1952.
5. ——, The logical basis of factor analysis. *Amer. Psychol.*, **8,** 105–114, 1953.
6. ——, *The Structure of Human Personality.* London: Methuen, 1953.
7. FRANKS, C., An Experimental Study of Conditioning as Related to Mental Abnormality. Unpublished doctor's dissertation, University of London Library, 1954.
8. FRASER, R., *The Incidence of Neurosis among Factory Workers.* London: H.M.S.O., 1947.
9. GIBSON, J. J., Adaptation, after-effect and contrast in the perception of curved lines. *J. exp. Psychol.*, **16,** 1–51, 1933.
10. GROSS, O., *Die cerebrale Sekundärfunction.* Leipzig: Vogel, 1902.
11. ——, *Über psychopathologische Minderwertig-Keiten.* Leipzig: Vogel, 1909.
12. GUILFORD, J. P., *An Inventory of Factors STDCR.* Beverly Hills, California: Sheridan Supply Company, 1942.
13. HILDEBRAND, H. P., A Factorial Study of Introversion-Extraversion by Means of Objective Tests. Unpublished doctor's dissertation, University of London Library, 1953.
14. HILGARD, E. R., JONES, L. V. & KAPLAN, S. J., Conditioned dis-

crimination as related to anxiety. *J. exp. Psychol.*, **42,** 94–99, 1951.

15. HOTELLING, H., The generalization of 'Student's' ratio. *Ann. math. Statist.*, **2,** 360–368, 1931.
16. HOYT, C., Test reliability obtained by analysis of variance. *Psychometrika*, **6,** 153–160, 1941.
17. HULL, C. L., *Principles of Behaviour.* New York: D. Appleton-Century, 1943.
18. KLEIN, G. S. & KRECH, D., Cortical conductivity in the brain-injured. *J. Pers.*, **21,** 118–148, 1952.
19. KÖHLER, W. & DINNERSTEIN, D., Figural aftereffects in kinesthesis. In: *Miscellanea Psychologica* (ed. Albert Michotte). Louvain: Institut Superieur de Philosophie, 1947.
20. —— & WALLACH, H., Figural after-effects: an investigation of visual processes. *Proc. Amer. phil. Soc.*, **88,** 269–357, 1944.
21. KONORSKI, J., *Conditioned Reflexes and Neuron Organization.* Cambridge: Cambridge University Press, 1948.
22. LANDIS, C., *An Annotated Bibliography of Flicker Fusion Phenomena.* Michigan: Michigan Armed Forces-National Research Council, 1953.
23. LUCHINS, A. S. & LUCHINS, E. H., The satiation theory of figural after-effects and Gestalt principles of perception. *J. Gen. Psychol.*, **49,** 3–29, 1953.
24. MCLEOD, H., An Experimental Study of the Inheritance of Introversion-Extraversion. Unpublished doctor's dissertation, University of London Library, 1954.
25. OSGOOD, C. E. & HEYER, A. W., A new interpretation of figural after-effects. *Psychol. Rev.*, **59,** 98–118, 1952.
26. PAVLOV, I. P., *Lectures on Conditioned Reflexes.* Vol. II. London: Lawrence & Wishart, 1941.
27. ——, *Conditioned Reflexes.* London: Oxford University Press, 1927.
28. PETRIE, A., *Personality and the Frontal Lobes.* London: Routledge & Kegan Paul, 1952.
29. —— & LE BEAU, J., A comparison of the personality changes after (1) prefrontal selective surgery for the relief of intractable pain and for the treatment of mental cases; (2) cingulectomy and topectomy. *J. ment. Sci.*, **99,** 53–61, 1935.
30. —— & ——, Études psychologiques des changements de la personalité produits par certaines opérations préfrontales sélèctives. *Rev. de Centre de Psychol. appl.*, **4,** No. 1, 1–16, 1953.

31. —— & ——, Psychological effects of selective frontal surgery including cingulectomy. *Proc. Vth Int. Congr. Neurol.*, Lisbon, **4,** 392–395, 1953.
32. Rawdon-Smith, A. R. R., Experimental deafness. Further data upon the phenomenon of so-called auditory fatigue. *Brit. J. Psychol.*, **26,** 233–244, 1936.
33. Reese, W. G., Doss, R. & Gantt, W. H., Autonomic responses in differential diagnoses of organic and psychogenic psychoses. *AMA Arch. Neurol. Psychiat.*, **70,** 778–793, 1953.
34. Rim, Y. S., Perseveration and Fluency as Measures of Extraversion-Introversion in Abnormal Subjects. Unpublished doctoral dissertation, University of London Library, 1953.
35. Sampson, H. & Bindra, D., 'Manifest' anxiety, neurotic anxiety and the rate of conditioning. *J. abnorm. soc. Psychol.*, **49,** 256–259, 1954.
36. Shapiro, M. B., Experimental studies of a perceptual anomaly. *J. ment. Sci.*, **97,** 90–110, 1957.
37. ——, Experimental studies of a perceptual anomaly. II. Confirmatory and explanatory experiments. *J. ment. Sci.*, **98,** 605–617, 1951.
38. ——, Experimental studies of a perceptual anomaly. III. The testing of an explanatory theory. *J. ment. Sci.*, **99,** 393–410, 1953.
39. ——, An experimental investigation of the block design rotation effect. An analysis of psychological effect of brain damage. *Brit. J. med. Psychol.*, **27,** 84–88, 1954.
40. ——, A preliminary investigation of the effects of continuous stimulation on the perception of 'apparent motion'. *Brit. J. Gen. Psychol.*, **45,** 58–67, 1954.
41. Spearman, C., *The Abilities of Man.* London: Macmillan, 1927.
42. Taylor, J. A., The relationship of anxiety to the conditioned eyelid response. *J. exp. Psychol.*, **41,** 81–92, 1951.
43. —— & Spence, K. W., The relationship of anxiety level to performance in serial learning. *J. exp. Psychol.*, **44,** 61–64, 1952.
44. Thurstone, L. L., *Multiple Factor Analysis: a Development and Expansion of the Vectors of the Mind.* Chicago: University of Chicago Press, 1947.
45. Welch, L. & Kubis, J., The effect of anxiety on the conditioning rate and stability of the PGR. *J. Psychol.*, **23,** 83–91, 1947.
46. —— & ——, Conditioned PGR (psychogalvanic response) in states of pathological anxiety. *J. nerv. ment. Dis.*, **105,** 372–381, 1947.

12

Personality and Reminiscence—An Experimental Study of the 'Reactive Inhibition' and the 'Conditioned Inhibition' Theories

H. J. EYSENCK[1]

First published in *Life Sciences*, **3,** 189–198, 1964

INTRODUCTION

IN a previous article (Ref. 7) Eysenck has proposed a three-factor theory of reminiscence, involving reactive inhibition (temporary work decrement), conditioned inhibition (permanent work decrement) and consolidation (perseveration). It was also postulated that experimental tasks differed greatly among themselves with respect to the degree to which these factors were involved; thus pursuit rotor learning was suggested to give rise to reminiscence scores dependent almost purely on consolidation, while vigilance tasks depended far more on reactive inhibition and the dissipation of reactive inhibition. Fig. 70 is quoted from the above-mentioned article to show the precise difference between the inhibition and the consolidation theories. According to the former, point B is depressed by inhibition-produced performance decrement, the dissipation of which raises C above B after rest; according to the latter, consolidation takes place during the rest, thus raising C above B. Evidence was found in the article for the importance of the consolidation variable in pursuit rotor learning and also for the belief that pursuit rotor learning was situated at one extreme of the continuum extending to vigilance tasks of the other extreme (Ref. 7).

The postulation of a continuum of this kind throws some light on a very important correlate of reminiscence, namely the personality trait of extraversion-introversion. The writer has postulated that extraverts are characterized by strong inhibitory and weak excitatory potentials and has also proposed that this hypothesis could be tested by means of

[1] The writer is indebted to the Maudsley and Bethlem Royal Hospital Research Fund for the support of this investigation. He is also grateful to Mr C. Atwood for kindly allowing him to test apprentices at the Ford works at Dagenham.

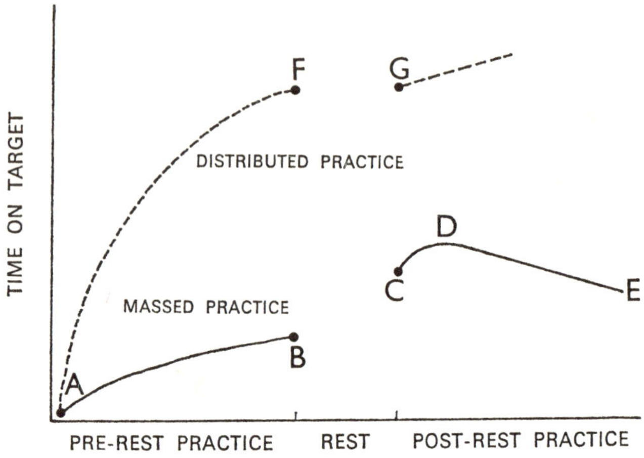

Figure 70. Shape of work curves under conditions of massed and distributed practice.

reminiscence experiments. This proposal was made on the basis of accepting the 'inhibition' theory of reminiscence, according to which reminiscence is a measure of the total amount of inhibition accumulated during pre-rest practice (Ref. 3). A survey of the available literature has disclosed that this prediction was in fact borne out, but that the correlations found were all disappointingly low (Ref. 4). It will be clear from our discussion above that pursuit rotor performance (which has been used in the great majority of these experiments) is far from being an ideal method for testing the personality theory in question, by virtue of the fact that reminiscence here is due almost entirely to consolidation and only to a very small degree to inhibition. Vigilance tests would appear to be far more suitable and indeed the evidence in this field is much more clear-cut and reliable than in the case of pursuit-rotor work. We thus derive from our consideration of the consolidation-inhibition continuum an important pointer regarding the choice of proper tests for the measurement of extraversion and for the testing of the general theory linking inhibition and extraversion.

It is interesting to consider why, precisely, investigations of reminiscence in pursuit rotor learning have usually discovered greater reminiscence in extraverted than in introverted subjects, in spite of the fact that we have shown reminiscence to be due to consolidation rather than to inhibition on this task. It could, of course, be postulated that extraverts learn better than do introverts and therefore improve more during the consolidation period; such an *ad hoc* postulate, however, would not link up with anything known about the experimental correlates of extraversion and introversion. It might also be thought that perhaps inhibition did play some part in the genesis of the reminiscence phenomenon, although rather less than did consolidation and that this small contribution was mirrored in the rather slight correlation usually found between reminiscence and extraversion. This hypothesis would demand that extraverts and introverts should differ in pre-rest performance at point B, but not at points A or C. Some support for such a view comes from the work of Ray (Ref. 11) and Bendig & Eigenbrode (Ref. 1).

An alternative theory is here presented which, while also accounting for the observed differences in reminiscence, would differ in certain testable ways from the theory just mentioned. According to the view defended in this article, we are dealing with a highly complex phenomenon in our work on reminiscence and the position of point C must be compared, not only with point B, but also with point G (Fig. 70) which shows the performance achieved by a group of subjects after an equivalent amount of practice *on a distributed practice schedule*. The fact that C falls short of G, in spite of the fact that maximum dissipation of inhibition has occurred (Ref. 10), or that maximum consolidation has taken place (Ref. 7), is due to the accumulation of conditioned inhibition ($_sI_R$). This conditioned inhibition arises because of the reinforcing effect of the 'blocks' or involuntary rest pauses which are the result of reactive inhibition building up to the level of the drive (D) under which the individual subject is working. These I.R.P.s, which have good experimental support in relation to many tasks, may or may not depress the actual level of performance, depending on certain properties of the task; it is here assumed that they do not depress performance on the pursuit rotor. Now it has been shown that introverts condition more quickly and more strongly than do extraverts (Ref. 5) and it might be predicted that in consequence they should also accumulate more $_sI_R$, which would depress their performance at point C. This would give rise to a difference in reminiscence between extraverts and introverts in the predicted direction, not because of poorer performance of extraverts at point B, but because of poorer performance of introverts at point C. Such an hypothesis is, of course, readily testable and an experiment along these lines will be reported presently.

Before doing so, however, we must deal with a theoretical objection to the scheme outlined above. According to our personality postulate, extraverts should have more I.R.P.s than introverts and Spielmann

(Ref. 12) and Eysenck (Ref. 8) have shown, in connection with a tapping task, that this is actually so. As level of conditioning is a function of number of reinforcements (in this case, I.R.P.s), we would, on these grounds, expect extraverts, rather than introverts, to develop greater conditioned inhibition. This is a serious objection and it is impossible to be certain that it is not fatal to our hypothesis. However, Eysenck has shown in a comparison of eye-blink conditioning records of extraverted and introverted subjects (Ref. 5), that 30 reinforcements for an extraverted group resulted in a level of performance roughly equal to that of an introverted group which had received only 3 or 4 reinforced trials. Even quite large differences in number of reinforcements may therefore be postulated to be incapable of overcoming the greater speed and strength of conditioning in introverted subjects, although it would, of course, require to be proved more directly that results obtained with eye-blink conditioning can indeed be taken over into a field of conditioning so very different in many ways.

A rather different objection might be raised on the grounds that at point B there is no differentiation between introverts and extraverts, although they are postulated to differ with respect to $_{S}I_{R}$ which is assumed to have a depressing effect; should not introverts be inferior in performance to extraverts at this point? The answer surely must be that according to the consolidation theory *all* habits require a rest pause after massed practice before learning can take place on any permanent basis; this must apply to $_{S}I_{R}$ just as much as to $_{S}H_{R}$. Consequently the differential effects of the growth of $_{S}I_{R}$ will not become apparent until *after* consolidation has taken place during the rest pause.

Experiment

211 male applicants for an apprenticeship training scheme were administered the pursuit rotor under conditions of high drive (Ref. 6); they were also administered the Eysenck Personality Inventory (E.P.I.) (Ref. 9), a modified and improved form of the M.P.I. This instrument provides scores on the two personality dimensions of Extraversion and Neuroticism; in the present experiment only the E scale (Form A) has been used. Of the subjects who had filled in the E.P.I., 23 could not be matched by name with pursuit rotor records (names were illegibly written, or initials did not match). Of the remainder, 28 had E scores of 16 and above; these will be called the extraverted group. 23 subjects had scores of 9 or below; these will be called the introverted group. (The standardization group for this test had a mean of 12·08 and a S.D.

of 4·37.) Very roughly, therefore, our two groups are about one S.D. above and below the mean for E.

The apprentices were all aged between 15 and 17 years and took the pursuit rotor test as part of a selection battery, not knowing that scores would not in fact contribute to their acceptance or rejection. All Ss practised for 5 minutes, rested for 10 minutes and practised for another 5 minutes. The apparatus and procedure have been described in detail elsewhere (Ref. 6). Practice was massed, recording being switched every 10 sec from one of the two clocks to the other, to enable the score to be read and recorded. The first post-rest trial was preceded by 2 sec of rotary pursuit, so that Ss should not enter the first trial 'cold', but would have an equal chance on this as on succeeding trials of starting off 'on target'. Standard instructions were given to all Ss and verbal correction applied if they did not act according to instructions. Scores were recorded to the nearest 0·01 sec. The reminiscence measure used subtracted the mean of the last three pre-rest scores from the mean of the first three post-rest scores.

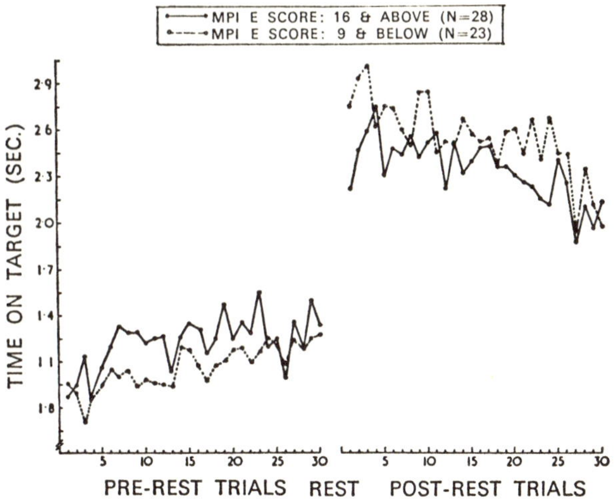

Figure 71. Pre-rest and post-rest performance of extraverted and introverted subjects on the pursuit rotor.

The performance of the two groups is plotted in Fig. 71 and it will be seen that as predicted the extraverts have a higher reminiscence score than do the introverts (1·67 as compared with 1·09). This difference is significant at the $p<0·05$ level, $t = 2·36$. It will also be seen that the two groups do not differ at all at point B (terminal pre-rest practice) but differ profoundly at point C (initial post-rest practice). These data are as predicted from the 'conditioned inhibition' hypothesis and contrary to the 'reactive inhibition' hypothesis. It will be remembered that these were 'high drive' apprentices and it might be thought that under conditions of low drive different results might be found. Star has produced a diagram (Ref. 13, Fig. 19) of the pursuit rotor performance of the 26 highest and lowest M.P.I. E scale scorers out of 100 low drive apprentices; the predicted differences in reminiscence are observed between phase 1 and phase 2 and it can be seen from the diagram that this is due entirely to post-rest performance superiority of the extraverted group, rather than to pre-rest superiority of the introverted group. (In fact, in his study the extraverted group shows a slight superiority in performance in their terminal pre-rest performance.)

Evidence from the literature, however, is by no means unanimous, although it is often impossible to decide because results are usually reported in terms of correlations between extraversion and reminiscence, thus obscuring the nature of the relationship. However, Eysenck's original data (Ref. 2) were still available for inspection; the extraverts show both a depressed pre-rest and an elevated post-rest performance, with the former contributing rather more to the total reminiscence score. The number of cases is, of course, too small to take this result too seriously (10 extraverts and 10 introverts), but in conjunction with the reported findings of Ray (Ref. 11) and Bendig & Eigenbrode (Ref. 1) the results do suggest that under certain as yet unspecified circumstances reactive inhibition may produce performance decrement on the pursuit rotor and thus contribute to the total reminiscence score. For the greater part, however, it may be suggested that reminiscence on this instrument is more likely to be due to greater conditioned inhibition on the part of introverted subjects, giving rise to lower post-rest performance.

DISCUSSION

The results of this experiment, while supporting the hypothesis that conditioned inhibition, rather than reactive inhibition, is responsible for reminiscence effects in pursuit rotor learning, do not of course directly support the particular hypothesis relating reminiscence to personality put forward in this article. It is entirely feasible to put forward alternative theories relating personality to learning, or to the consolidation process proper, rather than to the differential effects of conditioned inhibition. The only definite conclusion the experiment suggests in this connection is that the original hypothesis linking personality to reminiscence through individual differences in reactive inhibition (Ref. 2) is not tenable any longer and must be replaced by a theory taking into account the facts here discovered. It should not prove impossible to design adequate tests for the adequacy or otherwise of the alternative hypothesis here presented; enough is known about the shape of the acquisition of conditioning curve to suggest that the length of pre-rest practice should be an important parameter in linking personality and reminiscence. Short periods would be expected to show less relationship between these variables than longer periods and a comparison of the present results with those reported by Star shows that this is indeed so (Ref. 13). Star originally predicted that on the basis of the 'reactive inhibition' hypothesis shorter periods of pre-rest practice would give higher correlations between extraversion and reminiscence; his discovery of an opposite result could not be explained in terms of this hypothesis, but fits in well with the theory here outlined.

SUMMARY

28 extraverted Ss and 23 introverted Ss were administered the pursuit-rotor twice for 5 minutes, with a rest of 10 minutes intervening. Reminiscence scores were found to be significantly higher for the extraverted group. Plotting of the performance data showed that the observed differences were due to post-rest superiority in performance of the extraverts, as predicted by the 'conditioned inhibition' hypothesis and not to pre-rest inferiority of the extraverts, as predicted by the 'reactive inhibition' hypothesis. The results were interpreted in terms of the writer's three-factor theory of reminiscence.

REFERENCES

1. Bendig, A. W. & Eigenbrode, C. R., A factor analytic investigation of personality variables and reminiscence in motor learning. *J. abnorm. soc. Psychol.*, **62,** 698, 1961.
2. Eysenck, H. J., Reminiscence, drive and personality theory. *J. abnorm. soc. Psychol.*, **53,** 328-333, 1956.
3. ——, *Dynamics of Anxiety and Hysteri* London: Routledge & Kegan Paul, 1957.

4. ——, Reminiscence, drive and personality—revision and extension of a theory. *Brit. J. soc. clin. Psychol.*, **1,** 127–140, 1962.
5. ——, Conditioning and personality. *Brit. J. Psychol.*, **53,** 299–305, 1962.
6. ——, (ed.) *Experiments in Motivation.* Oxford: Pergamon Press, 1964.
7. ——, An experimental test of the 'inhibition' and consolidation theories of reminiscence. *Life Sci.*, **3,** 175–188, 1964.
8. ——, Involuntary rest pauses in tapping as a function of drive and personality. *Percept. mot. Skills*, **18,** 173–174, 1964.
9. —— & Eysenck, S., *Manual of the E.P.I.* London: University of London Press, 1964.
10. Kimble, G. A., An experimental test of a two-factor theory of inhibition. *J. exp. Psychol.*, **39,** 15–23, 1949.
11. Ray, O. S., Personality factors in motor learning and reminiscence. *J. abnorm. soc. Psychol.*, **59,** 199–202, 1959.
12. Spielmann, I., The Relation Between Personality and the Frequency and Duration of Involuntary Rest Pauses During Massed Practice. Unpublished Ph.D. thesis, University of London Library, 1963.
13. Star, K. H., An Experimental Study of 'Reactive Inhibition' and its Relation to Certain Personality Traits. Unpublished Ph.D. thesis, University of London Library, 1957.

13

Tolerance for Pain, Extraversion and Neuroticism[1]

R. LYNN & H. J. EYSENCK

First published in *Perceptual and Motor Skills*, **12,** 161–162, 1961

It may be deduced from Eysenck's theory of personality (Refs. 2 & 4) that pain tolerance should be *positively* related to extraversion (E) and *negatively* to neuroticism (N). Extraverted Ss are postulated to develop inhibition/satiation more quickly, and dissipate it more slowly; prolonged pain sensations should thus be inhibited more quickly and strongly in extraverts, leading to diminished pain sensations. Furthermore, as Beecher has pointed out, physiological pain sensations are always accompanied by the *apprehension of future pain*, which may be conceived as a conditioned fear (anxiety) response which summates with the physiological pain (Ref. 1). Extraverts are posited to condition less well, and would therefore not develop this component of the total pain to the same extent as introverts. The prediction relating to N is perhaps less secure; it rests on the assumption that the strength of the autonomic reaction to pain stimulation would be likely to be related directly to N, which is conceived of in terms of autonomic lability (Ref. 5). This autonomic reaction would be expected to summate with the physiological pain due to the stimulus.

30 volunteer university students, the experimental group, were given the Maudsley Personality Inventory as a measure of E and N (Ref. 3), as well as the Rotating Spiral After-effect test which is an objective measure of E (Ref. 4). Ss' foreheads were blackened with indian ink, and they were then subjected to heat stimulation by a thermostimulator modelled after the description given by Hardy, Wolff & Goodell (Ref. 7). The radiation intensity was set at 166 w, and Ss were instructed to report the onset of pain, which is usually characterized by a sharp prick following a sensation of warmth. They were then to try to tolerate the pain for as long as they could. Pain tolerance was the number of seconds from the first report of pain to the final withdrawal. All Ss reported pain

[1] We are indebted to the Society for Research in Human Ecology for a grant which made this study possible.

within 3 to 5 sec after exposure. There appears to be a habituation effect after about 12 sec of pain, such that, if pain could be tolerated for this long, Ss reported that they felt it could be endured indefinitely. Five Ss tolerated the pain for 60 sec, after which the trial was terminated. A time limit of 20 sec was finally set because of blisters which began to develop after about 8 sec exposure.

When Ss are divided into three groups of 10 according to their E scores, their pain tolerance decreases from 17·2 (high E) through 9·3 to 5·6 (low E); in the most extraverted group 8 out of 10 reach the 20 sec limit, while in the most introverted group none do. Mean score for the whole group is 10·9 sec. The product-moment correlation of E with pain tolerance is 0·69 ($p = 0{\cdot}01$). The correlation of N with pain tolerance is −0·36 ($p = 0{\cdot}05$). The Spiral After-effect correlates −0·30 with E, −0·02 with N, and −0·08 with pain tolerance. None of these correlations is significant, although the first approaches significance.

The very positive findings regarding E duplicate those of Petrie (Ref. 8), Petrie, Collins & Solomon (Ref. 9) and Poser (Ref. 10). The latter used 18 female students, subjected to ischemic pain, and found a correlation of 0·53 with E, as measured on the M.P.I.; the former has also used the M.P.I. on 55 Ss subjected to surgical or experimental pain and has reported significant differences between extraverts and introverts. (She also verified a complementary prediction deriving from the hypothesis, to wit that *stimulus deprivation* would be better tolerated by introverts.) The extensive data of Hall & Stride (Ref. 6) on some 400 psychiatric patients may also be quoted in support; they found least pain tolerance in dysthymics, i.e., introverted neurotics. They also report an increase in tolerance after pre-frontal leucotomy, which is an *extraverting* operation (Ref. 11).

SUMMARY

Significant correlations were found between pain tolerance on the one hand, and extraversion and (low) neuroticism on the other. These results are in line with deductions from Eysenck's theory of personality and are supported by other studies reported in the literature.

REFERENCES

1. Beecher, H. K., *Measurement of Subjective Responses: Quantitative Effects of Drugs*. New York: Oxford Univ. Press, 1959.
2. Eysenck, H. J., *Dynamics of Anxiety and Hysteria*. New York: Praeger, 1957.
3. ——, *Manual of the Maudsley Personality Inventory*. London: Univ. of London Press, 1959.
4. —— (ed.), *Experiments in Personality*. (2 vols.) London: Routledge & Kegan Paul, 1960.
5. ——, *The Structure of Human Personality*. New York: Wiley & Sons, 1960.
6. Hall, K. R. L & Stride, E., The varying response to pain in psychiatric disorders: a study in abnormal psychology. *Brit. J. med. Psychol.*, **27**, 48–60, 1954.
7. Hardy, J. D., Wolff, H. G. & Goodell, H., *Pain Sensations and Reactions*. Baltimore: Williams & Wilkins, 1952.
8. Petrie, A., Some psychological aspects of pain and the relief of suffering. *Ann. N.Y. Acad. Sci.*, **86**, 13–27, 1960.
9. ——, Collins, W. & Solomon, P., The tolerance for pain and for sensory deprivation. *Amer. J. Psychol.*, **73**, 80–90, 1960.
10. Poser, E., Der Figurale After-effect als Persoenlichkeitsmerkmal: Theorie und Methodik. Paper read at the XVIth Int. Congr. of Exp. Psychol., Bonn, 1960.
11. Willett, R. A., The effects of psychosurgical procedures on behaviour. In *Handbook of Abnormal Psychology* (ed. H. J. Eysenck). New York: Basic Books, 1960.

14

Conditioning, Introversion-Extraversion and the Strength of the Nervous System

H. J. EYSENCK[1]

First published in
Proceedings of the 18th International Congress of Psychology, 9th Symposium, 1966

TEPLOV'S main contribution to psychology consisted of the systematic working out of the relations obtaining between personality on the one hand and the concepts of excitation and inhibition on the other (Ref. 10). The work carried out in our laboratories, too, has concerned itself very much with these relations (Ref. 1) and in spite of obvious differences in approach there have also been certain interesting similarities. In particular, it would seem that the Pavlovian notion of 'strong' and 'weak' nervous systems, which has formed the basis for most of Teplov's experimental work, bears a striking similarity to the notions of extraverted and introverted personality types, as they emerge from our own. The 'weak' personality type appears to resemble the introvert, the 'strong' personality type the extravert. Even if it is admitted that similarity does not imply identity, it is certainly striking that two quite independent approaches should issue in such closely related concepts (Ref. 6).

This similarity becomes even more apparent when we consider these personality types in terms of physiological and neurological concepts. Gray has translated the concepts used by Pavlov and Teplov into the language of modern neurophysiology and has shown that different degrees of arousal of the reticular formation can mediate all or most of the experimentally ascertained differences between 'weak' and 'strong' nervous systems (Ref. 10). In a similar manner, Eysenck has suggested a close relationship between reticular formation arousal thresholds and introversion-extraversion (Ref. 7). According to these theories, low thresholds of the ascending reticular activating system would be

[1] Thanks are due to the M.R.C. for the support of this investigation.

characteristic of the 'weak' nervous system and the introvert, high thresholds of the 'strong' nervous system and the extravert. Again, the synchronizing part of the reticular formation exerts an inhibitory influence on cortical activity and it may be supposed that low thresholds of this system characterize the extravert and the 'strong' nervous system. Little direct evidence is unfortunately available relating to these theories, but work on the E.E.G. (Ref. 6), on critical flicker fusion (Ref. 12) and in particular on drugs known to affect the reticular formation (Ref. 12) has on the whole borne out the general theory in a rather striking manner (Ref. 4).

Among the similarities resulting from experimental work perhaps the most impressive is that relating to sensory thresholds. The lower thresholds found in persons possessing a 'weak' nervous system constitute one of the most important proofs of the Teplov school for the correctness of their theories. As a direct consequence of their work and the hypothesis relating introversion to a 'weak' nervous system, several studies have recently been carried out in England to study sensory thresholds in introverts and extraverts. Using the Maudsley Personality Inventory (Ref. 2) as the measure of personality, Haslam has several times found a significantly lower pain threshold in introverts as compared with extraverts and Smith has similarly discovered lower auditory thresholds in introverts using the usual psychophysical methods as well as a forced-choice technique. These and other experiments, too numerous to mention, make it likely that the conceptions of our two schools are in fact closely related and that empirical work directly devoted to a verification of this hypothesis would be of considerable value.

One interesting contrast between the Russian and the English work has been the comparative neglect of direct measures of conditioning by Teplov, as compared with the large body of work reported on this topic by the Maudsley group (Ref. 6). We have used in the main the eyeblink conditioning experiment, in which a puff of air to the eye is the unconditioned stimulus (UCS) and a tone delivered over ear-phones the conditioned stimulus (CS). A summary of the work on this test and on GSR conditioning, carried out by us and also by various other experimenters, has shown that different investigators have reported very divergent results, some producing the predicted positive correlation between introversion and conditionability, others failing to find such a correlation. The failure of so many experiments to duplicate the results of our early studies, which gave very positive results, would appear to be due to their failure to duplicate the exact conditions of the tests carried out; as will be shown below, the general theory linking introversion with greater cortical arousal ('excitation') predicts in some detail the exact choice of parameters which alone would be expected to generate positive correlations between introversion and conditioning. In particular, it is proposed that the following three parameters are crucial and must be carefully selected and controlled in order to obtain positive results.

(1) Partial reinforcement favours introverts; 100 per cent reinforcement does not.

(2) Weak unconditioned stimuli favour introverts; strong UCS do not.

(3) Small CS–UCS intervals favour introverts; large US–UCS intervals do not.

Partial Reinforcement

Pavlov already pointed out that unreinforced trials produced inhibition and if we link the growth of inhibition with extraversion in particular, then clearly partial reinforcement will impede conditioning more in extraverts than in introverts (Ref. 1). Furthermore, there is direct evidence to link partial reinforcement with cortical inhibition along neurophysiological lines; as Magoun has pointed out:

> 'In each of the several categories of conditioned reflex performance in which Pavlov found internal inhibition to occur . . . recent electrophysiological studies have revealed features of hypersynchronisation and/or spindle bursting in the E.E.G.' (Ref. 14).

UCS Strength

It is well known that conditioning is in part a function of the strength of the UCS (and possibly of the CS also—Ref. 13). Given that introverts have lower sensory thresholds (and probably smaller difference thresholds as well) than extraverts, then objectively identical UCS would be subjectively stronger for them and should therefore produce stronger conditioned responses. UCS of too great strength, on the other hand, should produce 'protective inhibition' much earlier in introverts than in extraverts. It may further be surmised that UCS of low strength adapt quickly and thus produce inhibition; this growth of inhibition again should be stronger in extraverts than in introverts. There is direct experimental backing for the inhibitory action of weak UCS and of partial reinforcement in the work of Ross & Spence who conclude:

'Inhibition of performance is more readily accomplished under conditions of low puff strengths . . . The differences between the 100 per cent and 50 per cent reinforcement groups at high levels of puff strength require that considerable "inhibition" still be present with such puffs' (Ref. 15).

CS–UCS Interval

It is well known that optimal CS–UCS intervals in eye-blink conditioning centre around 500 msec, but no work appears to have been done on individual differences in this respect. The concept of reaction time is clearly relevant here; Gray has summarized the work of the Teplov school by saying that 'at stimulus intensities below that at which asymptotic reaction time is reached, the weaker the nervous system, the faster the reaction time'. By going below the 500 msec mark, we can insure that we go below the asymptotic value for conditioning, and under those conditions, particularly when allied with weak UCS, we would expect introverts to react better to short CS–UCS intervals than extraverts. Gray has reviewed the whole literature on these relations quite exhaustively (Ref. 10), including the work of Fuster (Ref. 9) and of Issac (Ref. 11) on the association with the reticular formation and there seems little doubt that the experimental findings mediate a relationship such as that proposed.

It follows from what has been said that the very divergent findings with respect to the proposed relationship between introversion and eyeblink conditioning which form such a prominent feature of the literature, including the Russian, are only to be expected, considering that many different variations of type of reinforcement, CS–UCS interval and strength of UCS and CS have been employed. The experiment to be reported here, which was carried out by A. Levey in the Maudsley Laboratory, was specially designed to throw light on the hypotheses outlined above, relating to the change in the relation between conditioning and introversion with change in the conditions of the experiment. Subjects were tested under all possible combinations of two conditions of reinforcement, two CS–UCS intervals and two UCS strengths; for each pair of conditions a prediction was made (which has already been outlined) as to which condition would favour the introverts as compared with the extraverts. The detailed conditions of testing were as follows: *Reinforcement schedule*—100 per cent reinforcement against 67 per cent reinforcement. *CS–UCS interval:* 500 msec vs. 400 msec. *UCS strength:* 6 pounds per square inch vs. 3 pounds per square inch.

Subjects were selected on the basis of the Maudsley Personality

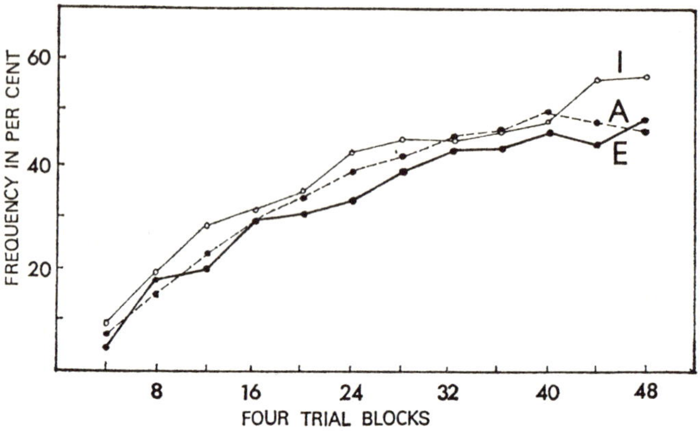

Figure 54. Rate of eyelid conditioning in extraverts, introverts and ambiverts under combination of all parameters.

Inventory and categorized as extraverted, introverted or intermediate (ambivert); they were also categorized as high, low or average on neuroticism. Equal numbers were then chosen from each of these categories, until 18 subjects had been included in each of the 8 experimental groups (combinations of reinforcement schedule, CS–UCS interval and UCS strength), making a total of 144 subjects in all; all of these were male. Fig. 54 shows the growth, over 48 acquisition trials, of conditioned habit strength for the extraverted, introverted and ambivert groups; there is a slight superiority of the introvert group over the extravert group in this overall comparison, amounting to some 20 per cent on the last few trials; the ambivert group is situated in between the other two groups most of the time, although it overlaps with both other groups on occasion. The differences are not significant on an analysis of variance, largely because of the tremendous size of the variances; this of course is not unexpected because of the variations in testing conditions imposed by our general scheme. Figs. 55 and 56 show the results for weak and strong UCS respectively; as expected the weak UCS shows introverts much more conditionable, while the strong UCS shows extraverts more conditionable. Ambiverts are intermediate between the two extreme groups. This reversal is quite dramatic and supports the prediction.

The results for the 400 and 800 msec CS–UCS interval show, as expected, that the short interval favours the introverts; for the long interval there is very little difference between the groups (Figs. 57 and 58). The

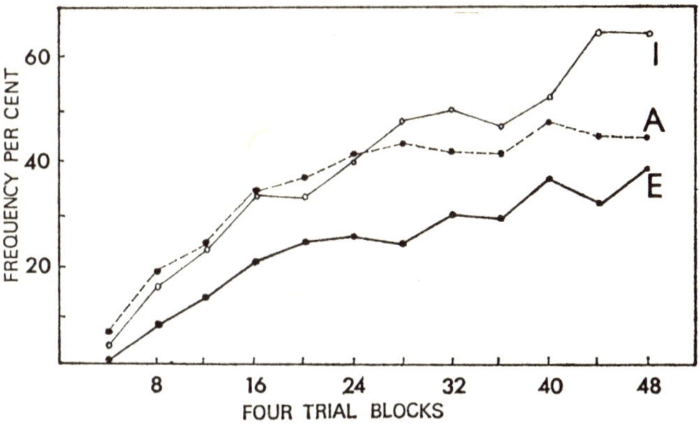

Figure 55. Rate of eyelid conditioning for introverts, ambiverts and extraverts under weak UCS conditions.

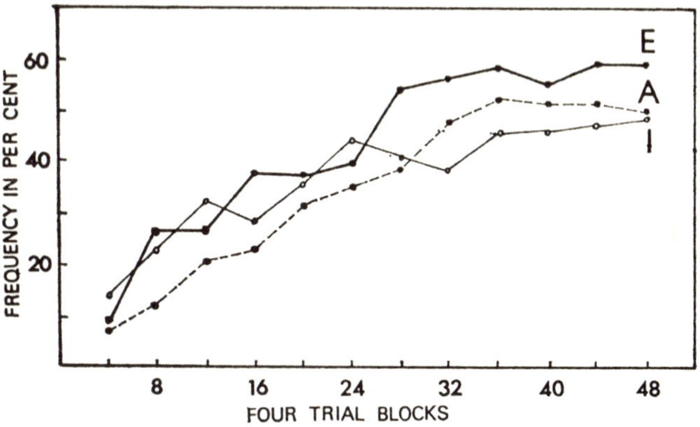

Figure 56. Rate of eyelid conditioning for extraverts, ambiverts and introverts under strong UCS conditions.

results for partial and continuous reinforcement show that there is a slight tendency for partial reinforcement to favour the introverts, but this tendency is not strong enough to give much support to our hypothesis (Figs. 59 and 60). If the results of this experiment can be taken as representative, we might conclude that strength of UCS was the most important parameter, followed by CS–UCS interval, with reinforcement schedule last. However, any such generalization would of course be restricted to the values of UCS strength, interval duration and reinforcement schedule adopted in this experiment; there is no reason to suppose that these are in any sense optimal. It seems very likely that much greater differences between introverts and extraverts could be demonstrated with better choice of parameter values. In particular, pressures of less than 3 pounds per square inch as UCS strength and intervals even shorter than 400 msec, present good prospects of improving discrimination.

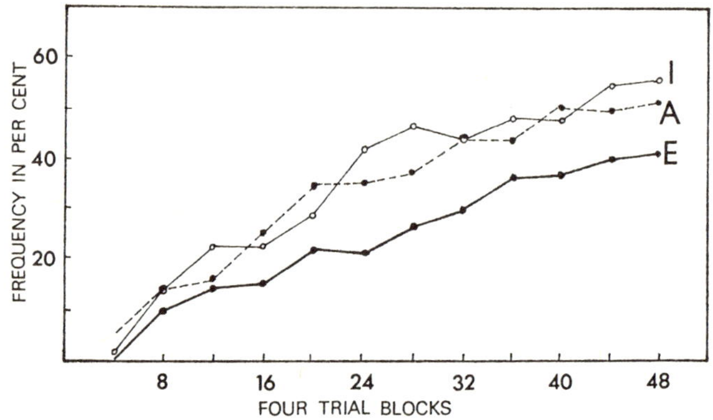

Figure 57. Rate of eyelid conditioning for introverts, ambiverts and extraverts under short CS-UCS interval conditions.

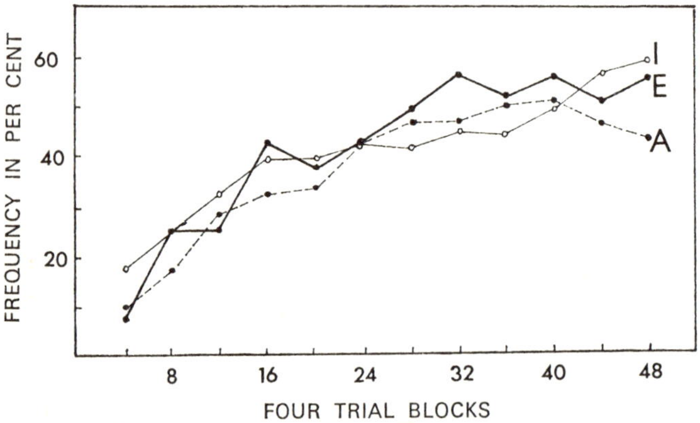

Figure 58. Rate of eyelid conditioning for extraverts, ambiverts and introverts under long CS-UCS interval conditions.

Figs. 61 and 62 present results for optimal and worst combinations of conditions respectively, i.e., weak UCS, short CS–UCS interval and partial reinforcement (Fig. 61) as against strong UCS, long CS–UCS

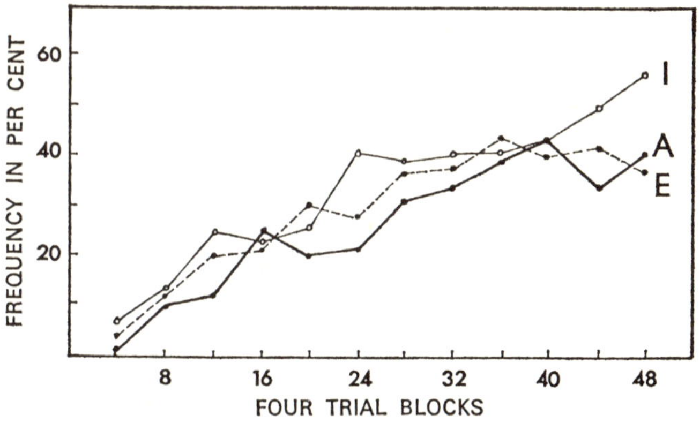

Figure 59. Rate of eyelid conditioning for introverts, ambiverts and extraverts under partial reinforcement conditions.

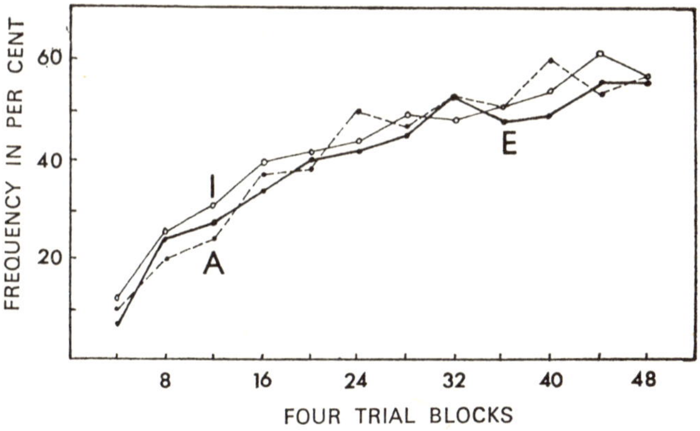

Figure 60. Rate of eyelid conditioning for extraverts, ambiverts and introverts under 100 per cent reinforcement conditions.

interval and continuous reinforcement (Fig. 62). The difference is obvious and may be summed up in the intra-group correlations. For the optimal conditions, the correlation between introversion and conditioning is +0·40, while for the worst conditions it is −0·31; this difference is significant at the 1 per cent level on a one-tail test. In the combination of conditions favourable, according to theory, to the introverts, we find that after 30 trials the extraverts show no evidence of any conditioning at all, while the introverts have reached a level of conditioning at which 46 per cent of responses are in fact conditioned. Conversely, under conditions favouring the extraverts, these produce after 30 trials almost twice as many conditioned responses as do the introverts.

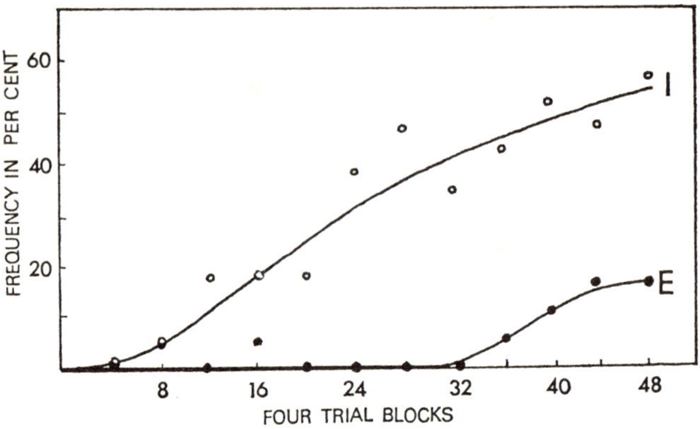

Figure 61. Rate of eyelid conditioning for introverts and extraverts under conditions of partial reinforcement, weak UCS, and short CS-UCS interval.

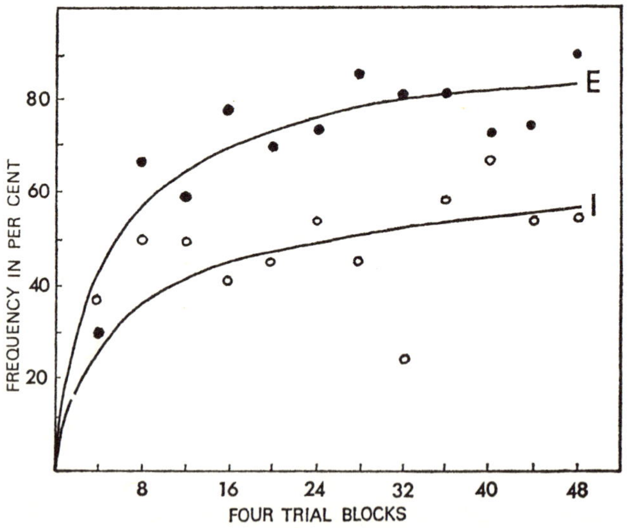

Figure 62. Rate of eyelid conditioning for extraverts and introverts under conditions of 100 per cent reinforcement, strong UCS, and long CS-UCS interval.

When we say that conditions are favourable to the introverted or the extraverted group, we are of course speaking in terms of comparison of the one group with the other. In fact there are many interesting comparisons to be made taking into account absolute levels of conditioning. Thus introverts achieve identical levels of conditioning at the end of the experiment (54 per cent), but they reach this end along quite different paths. (Fig. 63).

The introverts working under unfavourable conditions (as compared with extraverts) achieve a high level of conditioning very early (after 4 trials only) and do not change much after that; under favourable conditions (as compared to extraverts) they show a regular increase which gradually brings them up to the same level. Extraverts under favourable and unfavourable conditions behave quite differently (Fig. 64), as shown by the fact that the terminal values reached by them after 48 trials differ sharply; under unfavourable conditions, only 12 per cent condition, under favourable conditions, 92 per cent! If these data can be assumed to be generally valid, then it would seem that extraverts are much more at the mercy of conditions, while introverts ultimately reach reasonable levels of conditioning regardless of conditions. Replication of these results would seem to be desirable before too much effort is spent on explanations along theoretical lines. (It is interesting to note that the ambivert group shows very similar growth patterns under both conditions, namely the usual gradual increment in number of conditioned responses (Fig. 65). As might have been expected, the strong

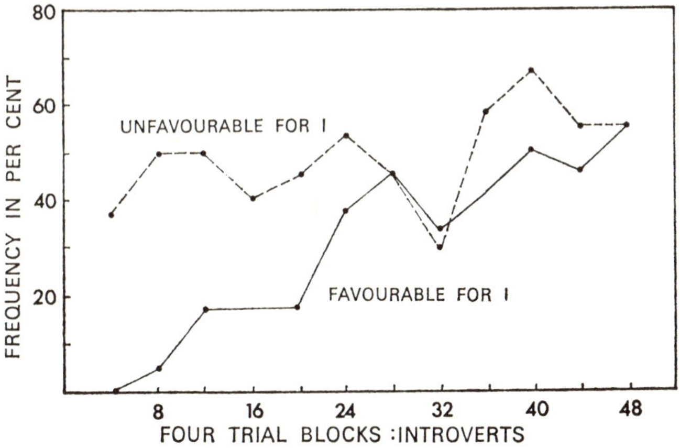

Figure 63. Rate of eyelid conditioning for introverts under conditions favourable and unfavourable for introverts.

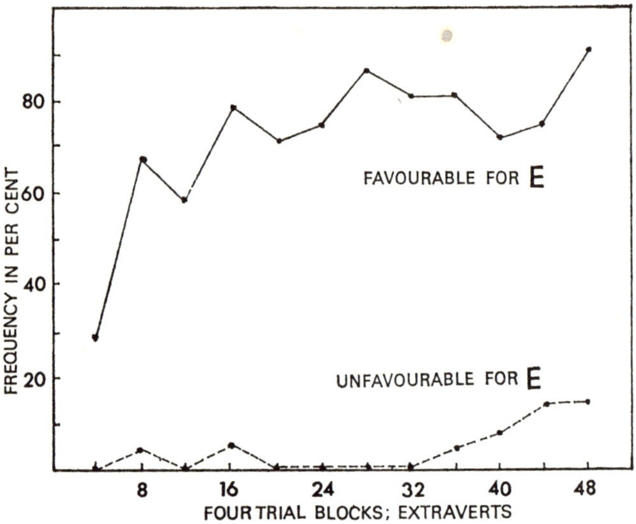

Figure 64. Rate of eyelid conditioning for extraverts under conditions favourable and unfavourable for extraverts.

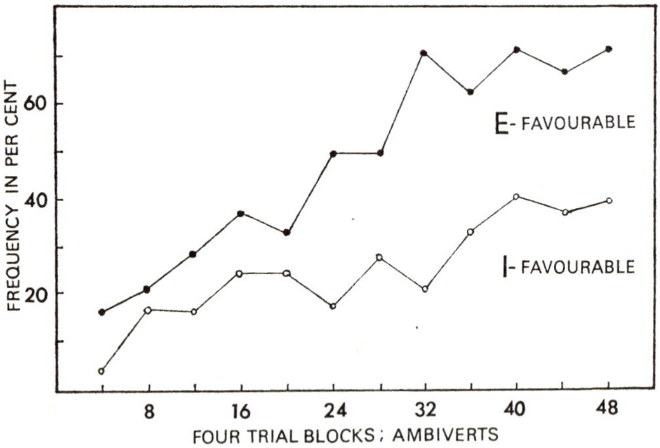

Figure 65. Rate of eyelid conditioning for ambiverts under conditions favourable for introverts and extraverts, respectively.

UCS-continuous reinforcement conditions result in better conditioning, but there is no dramatic difference in the shape of the curves; all that is apparent is a lower starting point and a less marked slope for the weak UCS-partial reinforcement conditions.)

In this case conditions may be said to be *overall* favourable or unfavourable according to the total amount of conditioning that takes place under these conditions for the total population tested. Thus strong UCS intensity produces quicker conditioning than does weak UCS intensity; 800 msec CS–UCS intervals are somewhat better than 400 msec intervals; continuous reinforcement is better than partial reinforcement. The results clearly show that the conditions which are favourable for the formation of conditioned responses *on the whole*, are, in this experiment at least, also those which are favourable to extraverts and unfavourable to introverts, respectively. One might be tempted to argue from these facts towards some general law of the kind: introverts form conditioned responses even under objectively unfavourable conditions; extraverts only form conditioned responses when conditions are optimal. Such a statement is in line with our results, but much more work along these lines will be required before we can regard it as well supported; clearly the particular selection of conditions of this one experiment and the inevitably small number of subjects tested, restrict the generality of our findings. Nevertheless, it may be useful to restate our major finding in this form, if only to suggest a possible link with clinical, penological and other applied fields (Refs. 1 & 5).

SUMMARY

It is now time to summarize the results obtained. As has been stressed before (Ref. 3), it is meaningless to compare groups of persons on a test of conditioning unless parameters are precisely specified and if individual differences are the subject matter of the experiment, then such parameters must be chosen in accordance with a specific theory. The fact that the literature is full of contradictory results, achieved with apparently random selection of parameters, reinforces this point. Our data show that it is possible to choose conditions which give results favouring introverted subjects or extraverted subjects; what is interesting and important is that these conditions could be formulated and stated on theoretical grounds, so that the experimental results serve to support and verify the theory. The overall failure of the experiment to show differences between introverts and extraverts at a reasonable level of significance is also in line with the hypothesis; when conditions are evenly balanced between favouring one group or the other, then averaging results over all conditions should not give results strikingly favouring one side. It should be noted that the conditions chosen were by no means extreme; it will be interesting to continue experimentation with more extreme conditions and thus render the differentiation of introverts and extraverts even more clear-cut and obvious than has been possible in the present experiment. It should also be interesting to continue work on eyeblink conditioning by linking it up with experimental measures of the Pavlov-Teplov dimension of weak-strong nervous system; predictions here are in general very similar to those made in connection with introversion-extraversion. Altogether it is believed that Pavlov was right in pointing out the fact that individual differences in conditioning are extremely prominent in work in this field and that these differences hold much promise in mediating predictions and explanations of human conduct, neurosis and crime. Efforts to do so (Refs. 1, 6 & 8) can only benefit from more intensive study of the relation between personality and different parameters of eyeblink conditioning.

REFERENCES

1. Eysenck, H. J., *The Dynamics of Anxiety and Hysteria.* London: Routledge & Kegan Paul, 1957.
2. ——, Conditioning and personality, *Brit. J. Psychol.*, **53,** 299–305, 1962.
3. ——, *The Maudsley Personality Inventory.* San Diego: Educ. Indust. Testing Service, 1959.
4. ——, The biological basis of personality. *Nature*, **199,** 1031–1034, 1963.
5. ——, *Crime and Personality.* Boston: Houghton-Mifflin, 1964.
6. ——, Extraversion and the acquisition of eyeblink and GSR conditioned responses. *Psychol. Bull.*, **63,** 258–270, 1965.
7. ——, *The Biological Basis of Personality.* Springfield: C. C. Thomas, 1967.
8. —— & Rachman, S., *Causes and Cures of Neurosis.* San Diego: R. R. Knapp, 1965.
9. Fuster, J. M., Effects of stimulation of brain stem on tachistoscopic perception. *Science*, **127,** 150, 1958.
10. Gray, J., *Pavlov's Typology.* Oxford: Pergamon Press, 1965.
11. Isaac, W., Arousal and reaction times in cats. *J. comp. physiol. Psychol.*, **53,** 234–236, 1960.

12. KILLAM, E. K., Drug actions on the brain stem reticular formation. *Pharmacol. Per.*, **14,** 175–224, 1962.
13. KIMBLE, G. A., *Hilgard and Marquis' Conditioning and Learning*. New York: Appleton-Century, 1961.
14. MAGOUN, H., *The Waking Brain*. Springfield: C. C. Thomas, 1963.
15. ROSS, L. E. & SPENCE, K. W., Eyelid conditioning performance under partial reinforcement as a function of UCS intensity. *J. exp. Psychol.*, **59,** 379–382, 1960.
16. SAVAGE, R. D., Electro-cerebral activity, extraversion and neuroticism. *Brit. J. Psychiat.*, **110,** 98–100, 1964.

15

Extraversion, Arousal, and Paired-Associate Recall

E. HOWARTH & H. J. EYSENCK

First published in
Journal of Experimental Research in Personality, **3,** 114–116, 1968

FROM a total of over 600 female Ss, 110 were selected with extreme extraversion scores. Fifty-five extraverts and 55 introverts were allocated among five recall intervals: 0, 1, 5, 30 min, 24 hrs in a 10-cell design. The subjects were first trained to a criterion of once through correct on seven CVC pairs, then were tested for recall of the material after the appropriate time interval. The results showed that extraverts were superior at the short-term intervals but inferior at the long-term intervals. These findings were interpreted in accord with Eysenck's theory that lower arousal in extraverts produces weaker consolidation processes which interfere less at short-term intervals but which do not facilitate long-term recall.

INTRODUCTION

Kleinsmith and Kaplan (Refs. 5 and 6) have demonstrated that associations learned in the presence of low arousal, as measured by skin resistance change, showed high immediate recall which fell over the course of several days, whereas items learned under high arousal showed poor immediate recall which improved with the passage of time. Walker and Tarte (Ref. 8) compared high arousal and low arousal stimuli and found a similar effect. It has been suggested, in connection with these findings, that high arousal produces strong consolidation which interferes with immediate recall in some way, but which facilitates later recall. Eysenck (Ref. 1) has proposed that extraverts have higher arousal thresholds in the brain-stem reticular system leading to lower arousal in the cortex. If this is correct they may be less affected by strong interfering consolidation in short-term recall and perform better, whereas introverts might perform poorly at short-term intervals but show good long-term recall. While there is little previous relevant work on paired-associates learning, Eysenck (Ref. 1) has used this theoretical formulation as a possible explanation of the higher reminiscence scores of extraverts in pursuitrotor learning after relatively short rest intervals and several other facets of the formulation have been confirmed by Farley (Ref. 3). Also, Howarth (Ref. 4) found that the short-term recall of extraverts was superior in a modified Wechsler digit-repetition task. The present study compares extraverts and introverts in a paired-associates recall task at time intervals up to and including 24 hr. On the basis of the theory it was predicted that extraverts would show greater recall at the short-term intervals and less recall at the long-term intervals, but it was impossible to define *a priori* the terms long and short term or to anticipate the kind of data which would emerge. For example, the arousal differences postulated in the theory might be far less marked, and therefore less effective, than those in the Kleinsmith and Kaplan study. Moreover, the differences observed by Walker at the shorter intervals were minimal.

METHOD

Subjects

In order to obtain extreme extraverts and introverts over 600 students were given the Eysenck Personality Inventory (Ref. 2) and 110 Ss were selected as being outside the range of ± 1 S*D*, on the E dimension at the same time those with neuroticism (N) scores greater than 17 were rejected in order to attenuate the possible effect of neuroticism. All Ss were female (except three) in the age range 18–22.

Material

Seven pairs of CVCs of medium association value (Ref. 7) were used in four orders of presentation. *One* of the four orders was as follows: SIP-WOL; VIL-MUF; GOP-FER; MEV-LAR; SEL-PON; MOT-PED; NOR-BEV. This material was presented by a Carousel projector cycled at 3 sec. The intertrial interval of 18 sec was occupied by colour-naming.

Instructions to S

'This is an experiment on the relation of learning and personality. You have already taken a personality test, we will now test your learning ability. The test consists of learning to associate word pairs. In each case pronounce each word as it appears, and as the trials progress show that you have learned the association by anticipating the response word. There are seven word pairs (example shown, but not from the series) but these will be in a different order on each trial, although the pairs will always remain the same. Between each series colours will be shown, do not learn the colours, simply name them as they appear.'

Learning and Recall Measures

(1) Learning of the list was to a criterion of once through correct.

(2) Recall of the material was carried out as follows: S was asked to 'print all the stimulus words, you can remember on the left-hand side of this line in any order you like, you have one minute.' Then S was asked to 'Now, print all the associated response words on the right-hand side of this line, pairing the correct response word to each stimulus word, you have one minute.' The recall score consisted of a combination (sum) of (*a*) all stimulus words correctly recalled (written down by S), and (*b*) all response words correctly reproduced by S, with the proviso that these should be correctly paired with the appropriate stimulus word.

Intervening Task

The S was instructed to make words of any length out of a longer word containing letters from which none of the CVC words could be made.

This method worked well up to the 30-min recall interval but could not be sustained at the 24-hr interval.

Experimental Design

This comprised ten cells (*a*) Two personality extremes (E vs. I) being randomly allocated among the five recall intervals (*b*) 0, 1, 5, 30 min, 24 hr.

RESULTS

As the results of the experiment were quite clear (Figure 1) the results section merely explains that (*a*) initial differences in learning rates were lacking, (*b*) the overall effect in the recall scores was significant. In initial learning the mean trials to criterion for the extraverts was 15·85, that for the introverts 18·29. This overall difference was not significant nor were the several group differences significant when a series of *t* tests was applied. Analysis of variance of the recall scores revealed a significant interaction effect between recall intervals and the E-I parameter ($F = 229$, $df = 4$, df for the error term $= 100$).

Mean recall scores are shown in Figure 1.

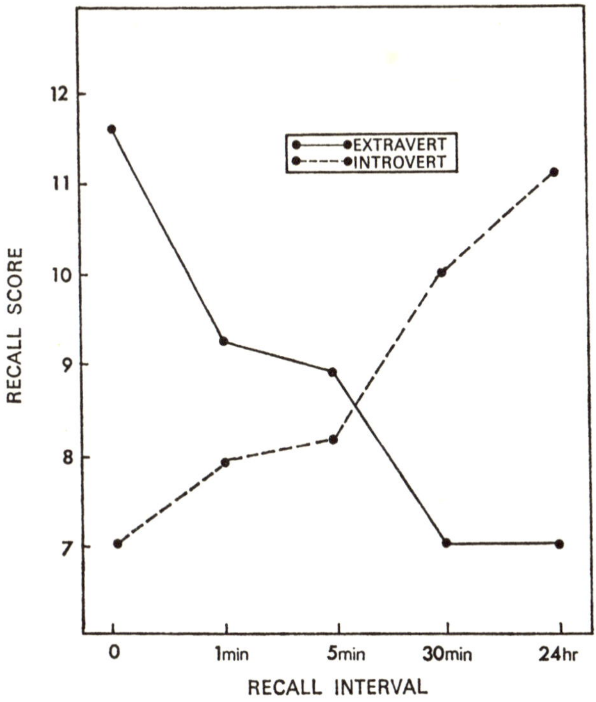

FIG. 1. Mean recall scores of extraverts and introverts at the recall interval stated. Maximum recall score possible was 14. Each is the mean score of 11 Ss.

DISCUSSION

According to Eysenck (Ref. 1) we could expect extraverts to be better at short-term intervals; 'conversely, we would expect introverts to show better serial learning, paired-associate learning and digit-span memory when the interval between learning and testing was relatively long.'

The results of this experiment are consistent with an expectation derived from the theoretical supposition of differences in arousal thresholds between extraverts and introverts. The general picture resembles that presented by the results of Kleinsmith and Kaplan except that their crossing point occurs at about 20 min, whereas that in the present experiment occurs at about 5 min, therefore for the purpose of the present study it appears convenient to define short-term recall as less than 5 min, and long-term recall as greater than this interval.

These findings, therefore, offer strong support for Eysenck's latest theoretical position regarding higher thresholds of arousal in extraverts. Combining this hypothesis with that of Walker, that retention is a function of consolidation of traces and that high arousal results in slower but more permanent consolidation, it follows that high arousal Ss should have poorer immediate recall but superior delayed recall. We have shown that, in this respect, extraverts behave as though they have lower arousal.

Although there is no previous evidence to support Eysenck's contention that long-term memory will be superior in introverts, there is some evidence (e.g. Ref. 4) to show that the short-term recall of extraverts is superior. However, there has been no previous study which compares extraverts and introverts in both short and long recall performance.

REFERENCES

1. EYSENCK, H. J., *The Biological Basis of Personality.* Springfield: Thomas, 1967.
2. —— & EYSENCK, S. B. G., Manual of the Eysenck Personality Inventory. R. R. Knapp, P. O. Box 7234, San Diego, California, 1964.
3. FARLEY, F. H., Reminiscence and post-rest performance as a function of length of rest, drive and personality. University of London Doctoral thesis, 1966.
4. HOWARTH, E., Some laboratory measures of extraversion-introversion. *Percept. Mot. Skills*, **17**, 55–60, 1963.
5. KLEINSMITH, L. J. & KAPLAN, S., Paired-associate learning as a function of arousal and interpolated interval. *J. exp. Psychol.*, **65,** 190–193, 1963.
6. ———, Interaction of arousal and recall interval in nonsense syllable and paired-associate learning. *J. exp. Psychol.*, **67,** 124–126, 1964.
7. NOBLE, C. E., Measurements of association value, rated association and scaled meaningfulness for the 2100 CVC combinations of the English alphabet. *Psychol. Rep.*, **8,** 487–521, 1961.
8. WALKER, E. L. & TARTE, R. D., Memory storage as a function of arousal and time with homogeneous and heterogeneous lists. *J. Verbal Learn. & Verbal Behav.*, **2,** 113–119, 1963.